Mentoring Student Teachers and Interns

Mentoring Student Teachers and Interns

Strategies for Engaging, Relating, Supporting, and Challenging Future Educators

Third Edition

Lawrence Lyman, Harvey C. Foyle,
Michael A. Morehead, Sara Schwerdtfeger,
and
Allyson L. Lyman

ROWMAN & LITTLEFIELD
Lanham • Boulder • New York • London

Published by Rowman & Littlefield
A wholly owned subsidiary of The Rowman & Littlefield Publishing Group, Inc.
4501 Forbes Boulevard, Suite 200, Lanham, Maryland 20706
www.rowman.com

Unit A, Whitacre Mews, 26-34 Stannary Street, London SE11 4AB

Copyright © 2017 by Lawrence Lyman, Harvey C. Foyle, Michael A. Morehead, Sara Schwerdtfeger, and Allyson L. Lyman

All rights reserved. No part of this book may be reproduced in any form or by any electronic or mechanical means, including information storage and retrieval systems, without written permission from the publisher, except by a reviewer who may quote passages in a review.

British Library Cataloguing in Publication Information Available

Library of Congress Cataloging-in-Publication Data Available

ISBN: 978-1-4758-3369-0 (cloth : alk. paper)
ISBN: 978-1-4758-3370-6 (pbk. : alk. paper)
ISBN: 978-1-4758-3371-3 (electronic)

∞™ The paper used in this publication meets the minimum requirements of American National Standard for Information Sciences—Permanence of Paper for Printed Library Materials, ANSI/NISO Z39.48-1992.

Printed in the United States of America

Contents

Foreword		vii
Acknowledgments		ix
Introduction		xi
1	Creating and Sustaining Productive Partnerships	1
2	Building Positive Relationships	13
3	Student Teaching Program Assessment and Accountability	27
4	Planning and Sequencing	39
5	Supervising the Intern	57
6	Helping Interns Succeed in Diverse Classrooms	73
7	The Struggling Intern	89
8	The Excellent Intern	101
9	The Principal's Role	109
10	Training for Mentor Teachers and University Supervisors	119
Appendix 1: Feedback for Applying What You Have Learned Videos		127
Appendix 2: Observable Instructional Behaviors to Reinforce		139

Appendix 3: Example of a Professional Development
    School Agreement   145

Appendix 4: Example of an Intern Improvement Contract   149

Selected Bibliography   153

Index   159

About the Authors   167

Foreword

Mentoring Student Teachers and Interns: Strategies for Engaging, Relating, Supporting, and Challenging Future Educators by Larry Lyman, Harvey Foyle, Michael Morehead, Sara Schwerdtfeger, and Allyson Lyman is a dynamic new book that builds upon more than three decades of collaborative practices for preparing those who wish to enter the teacher profession. These authors have devoted their careers to education and educating individuals who wish to join the ranks of P–12 educators through serving as classroom teachers and administrators and as teacher education faculty members in university settings.

In addition to providing specific strategies for effective and supportive student teacher and intern supervision, this book also includes chapters focusing on working with struggling student teachers, and preparing teacher candidates for the challenges of diverse schools and classrooms. The importance of ongoing communication between the cooperating/mentor teachers, university supervisors, and student teachers/interns including effective conferencing and assessment is addressed in multiple chapters.

Hyperlinks and YouTube videos provide examples and illustrations that further elaborate how to implement successful support and supervision for future educators engaged in clinical experiences in P–12 classrooms. Strategies for developing successful partnerships between P–12 schools, community colleges, and university teacher preparation programs receive special emphasis in this book.

A "must-read" for teachers and administrators in P–12 schools as well as community college and university faculty members who are actively engaged in preparing future educators, the authors summarize "tried and true" practices presented at regional, national, and international professional conferences with commendations for the practical ideas and "wisdom of practice" provided. The clarity and relevance of the topics included in this book will promote the preparation of well-prepared teachers for twenty-first-century classrooms!

Tes Mehring, PhD
Interim Provost
Baker University

Acknowledgments

The authors would like to recognize and thank the educators who have contributed to this publication:

The Mentor Teachers, University Supervisors, and other educators who have participated in our training sessions, presentations, and workshops from 1988–2016.

Robert Bingham	Dan Lumley
Stephanie Brockman	Tes Mehring
Marc Childress	Robert Owens
Tara Davis	Brooke Province
Joyce Didde	Matt Seimears
Carlos Galiano	Jack Skillett
Karen Hurla	Kaye Tague
Harriet Johnson	Charmetra Walker
Scott Kickhafer	Bill Warner
Frank Leone	Ken Weaver

Special thanks to Tom Koerner, Rowman & Littlefield, for his guidance and support with all three editions of this publication; Ashley Peterson, Emporia State University, who assisted with this revised edition; Nicole A. Hughes, New Mexico State University, who assisted in editing the second edition; Candace J. Sitzer, New Mexico State University, who assisted in editing, researching, and guiding the development of the first edition; and Tatiana Pachkova, research assistant in the graduate school at Emporia State University, 2000–2001, who assisted with the first edition.

Introduction

Mentoring Student Teachers and Interns: Strategies for Engaging, Relating, Supporting, and Challenging Future Educators is a substantially new interactive version of the previous work, *Working with Student Teachers: Getting and Giving the Best*. This revised book is intended to help university supervisors and mentor teachers to make the clinical experience successful and productive for the interns with whom they work. This book can also be used by field placement programs as a training resource for mentor teachers and supervisors.

Teachers who have the knowledge, skills, and dispositions to help students at all levels succeed are essential to school improvement efforts. It is the position of the authors of this book that these clinical experiences are most effective in Professional Development School settings. For this reason, we refer to the preservice teacher as an "intern," to the teachers in school settings who work with interns as "mentor teachers," and the university personnel who work with them during their clinical assignments as "supervisors."

In this interactive volume, we have provided hyperlink resources which support the ideas in each chapter, enhance the ideas with additional resources, and assist the mentor teacher and supervisor by providing resources that can be helpful to use with interns who need help with specific skills and topics. All hyperlinks were appropriate and were working at the time of publication.

In addition, video segments now are included for each chapter to provide an opportunity for the reader to apply the concepts and ideas of the chapter and to see examples of exemplary models. The videos can also be used as part of a training program for mentor teachers and supervisors. Feedback for each of the video tasks can be found in Appendix 1. The video segments include some that have been used for many years by the original authors of this book in training sessions with mentor teachers and supervisors and presentations to field placement program directors, public school administrators, and university administrators. New videos, prepared especially for this edition, are also included.

Chapter 1 focuses on how effective partnerships are created and sustained between local education agencies and university programs that prepare teachers. Two video segments included in the chapter focus on exemplary partnership models and the characteristics that have made the partnerships effective.

Chapter 2 analyzes the importance of building positive relationships between interns and their mentor teachers and supervisors. One of the critical components of positive and productive relationships is trust and suggestions are provided for building and sustaining trust, even when dealing with difficult issues. The video segments which accompany this chapter show how a supervisor deals with difficult issues effectively while maintaining trust.

Chapter 3 discusses the importance of assessment as part of the clinical experience. It is imperative that all stakeholders understand the assessments which are used in the program and how to utilize the assessments appropriately. Data from these assessments should be systematically used to enhance the quality of the program. The video segments for this chapter include a mentor and supervisor training session where a facilitator provides practice on using an assessment in a creative, engaging way. Another segment models a summative conference between an intern and mentor teacher at the end of the intern's experience.

Chapter 4 provides suggestions for planning and sequencing the intern's experience. Important topics in this chapter include introducing the intern into the classroom setting and beginning the teaching experiences. Video segments for this chapter offer examples of beginning and ending conferences with interns and suggestions for mentor teachers and supervisors about what to include in these conferences.

Chapter 5 identifies strategies for effective supervision of interns. The importance of formative and summative conferences with the intern and how to conduct these conferences successfully are discussed. Video segments provide examples of formative conferences with an intern in which the supervisor encourages the intern to actively participate in the conference and gives the intern feedback on her teaching.

Chapter 6 recognizes that diverse student populations have a profound effect on classrooms today. While teacher education programs emphasize diversity as part of their curriculum, interns may struggle with applying the concepts and strategies they have learned in actual classroom settings. Hyperlinks in this chapter provide resources which mentors and supervisors may use to help interns who struggle with interacting with students, equitable teaching practices, making appropriate adaptations, accommodating different

learning preferences, and using activities which motivate students. The video segments for this chapter identify challenges interns face when working with diverse students and examples of strategies interns use to succeed with diverse students.

Chapter 7 explores an issue of real concern for most mentor teachers and supervisors: the intern who struggles during the clinical experience. Strategies for working with struggling interns and the importance of following due process procedures are among the important topics in this chapter. The video segments in this chapter include examples of conferences with struggling interns and what components make such conferences effective.

Chapter 8 encourages mentor teachers and supervisors who work with excellent interns to continue to challenge these interns to grow professionally. Strategies for working with excellent interns such as the intern who does not utilize her skills to the fullest are discussed. The video segments for this chapter are examples of conferences with excellent interns to encourage reflection and problem solving.

Chapter 9 spotlights the role of the building principal in modeling the attitudes and setting the tone for acceptance of interns in a school. The degree of importance given to interns by the administrator encourages all members of the school community to view interns with acceptance and support. In the video segment for this chapter, a principal who has considerable experience with interns, mentor teachers, and university supervisors reflects on the benefits for his school of working with interns.

Chapter 10 is a new chapter designed for this revised edition. Components of effective training and strategies for designing training programs that actively involve participants are featured. Video segments provide specific examples of training activities which utilize different strategies to help mentor teachers and supervisors acquire the skills needed to work effectively with interns. As with all of the materials in this book, those charged with the responsibility for training mentors and supervisors are encouraged to adapt these ideas to the needs of their programs.

Appendices are provided with additional resources that may be helpful. As discussed, Appendix 1 provides feedback for the Apply What You Have Learned video tasks included in each chapter. Appendix 2 includes a list of observable instructional behaviors which can be productively reinforced by mentor teachers and supervisors. Appendix 3 is an example of a Professional Development School agreement between a university and a school district. Appendix 4 contains an example of a contract for improvement for a struggling intern. A bibliography of selected references follows the appendices.

Clinical experiences, such as those found in Professional Development Schools, offer much promise in preparing future teachers to be successful in today's challenging classrooms. As the title of the book indicates, in order to realize the potential benefits of PDS programs and other clinical programs for preservice teachers, mentor teachers and university supervisors must have the skills needed to engage with, relate to, support, and challenge future educators.

Chapter One

Creating and Sustaining Productive Partnerships

ADVANTAGES OF PRODUCTIVE PARTNERSHIPS

Partnerships between educators representing various agencies and constituencies involved in the preparation of new teachers can have many advantages. Increasing the amount of time spent in clinical settings, such as professional development schools, provides hands-on experiences that help future teachers to practice and refine their teaching skills. Additional input into program design, curriculum, and assessment from sources outside the university helps to increase the relevance of teacher education preparation and prepares future teachers for the *real world* of teaching.

Recent national reports on the quality of teacher education have raised concerns about how well beginning teachers are being prepared for the challenges they will face. According to the *Educating School Teachers*[1] report, "the nation's teacher education programs are inadequately preparing their graduates to meet the realities of today's standards-based, accountability-driven classrooms, in which the primary measure of success is student achievement." A more recent study by the National Council on Teacher Quality[2] raised similar concerns about teacher preparation.

Partnerships between universities and school districts can improve the preparation future teachers receive, by improving the quality and quantity of feedback they receive and by helping to assure that the clinical experiences of future teachers are as productive and positive[3] as possible. Partnerships can provide opportunities for colleagues to evaluate the effectiveness of teacher education initiatives and make needed changes and improvements. Opportunities to work together as partners can make effective use of limited resources and improve the quality of teacher preparation.

CHARACTERISTICS OF PRODUCTIVE PARTNERSHIPS

Sense of Mission

Educators in productive partnerships have a sense that collaborating together is necessary to address urgent needs. In the case of teacher education, partnerships can work together to address issues that may include the following:

- Preparation of teachers to meet the needs of increasingly diverse students.
- Preparation of teachers to implement multiple, effective teaching strategies.
- Recruitment of new teachers to meet the needs of growing school populations and retiring teachers.
- Recruitment of minority teachers.
- Recruitment of teachers for high-needs areas.
- Reducing attrition of beginning teachers in the first three to five years of teaching.
- Addressing public concerns about the quality of P–12 education and about teacher preparation.
- Reducing the cost of completing a teacher education program for future teachers.

Shared Goals and Vision

An important part of a productive partnership is the articulation of the common goals and beliefs[4] shared by the educators in the partnership. The development of specific goals, accompanied by desired outcomes and assessment strategies, is the first task of any productive partnership effort. Agreement on the roles and responsibilities of those involved is necessary to ensure the success of the partnerships.

Time

In partnerships that are productive, there is a willingness to spend the time necessary to collaboratively analyze teacher education and subject matter standards to determine how the desired outcomes of the standards can be most productively achieved. Creating a cohesive, aligned teacher education curriculum that maximizes the time the future teacher spends in a clinical setting working with students requires careful planning and flexibility. Time is also required to evaluate the effectiveness of the partnership. Such evaluation requires the analysis of data, discussion of positive and negative results, and planning for improvement.

Mutual Respect

Productive partnerships between educational agencies are characterized by mutual respect between the educators involved. Each of the constituencies involved in the partnership must respect the professionalism and expertise of the others. Because partnership efforts often involve changes that can seem uncomfortable or threatening to some participants, respect for the comfort levels, personalities, and professional concerns of colleagues is essential. Disagreements, which will inevitably occur when working together, must be resolved in positive, creative ways that respect the dignity of all involved.

Restructuring

In partnerships that are productive, resources are creatively and appropriately shared. Facilities, supplies, and personnel are among the resources that can be analyzed to determine the most efficient and effective way to meet the needs of future teachers.

Administrative Support

The support of the administrators from all agencies involved in partnerships is essential. Productive partnerships are sanctioned, encouraged, and supported with appropriate resources. Collaborative partnerships are encouraged and rewarded.

Celebration

Successful collaboration requires celebration of successes achieved as a result of partnership efforts. It is especially important, given the amount of negative publicity about schools and colleges of teacher education, that successful efforts to enhance the quality of teacher preparation and the success of P–12 students be celebrated and disseminated.

PROFESSIONAL DEVELOPMENT SCHOOL PARTNERSHIPS

Professional Development Schools (PDS) have emerged as one of the most promising partnerships[5] between university and P–12 educators. Table 1.1 summarizes the outcomes from successful PDS programs.

The National Association for Professional Development Schools identifies nine essential components[6] of effective PDS partnerships. For example,

Table 1.1. Desired Outcomes of Professional Development School Partnerships

The professional development school improves the preparation of future teachers.

The professional development school offers professional development opportunities for P–12 teachers.

The professional development school offers professional development opportunities for university faculty.

The professional development school positively affects the achievement of P–12 students.

using these nine essential components of a PDS partnership, Emporia State University utilized one university, two community colleges, and forty-five elementary schools in the eastern Kansas area to create successful PDS partnerships.[7]

PDS partnerships offer interns many opportunities to interact with students, and they also provide extended time to practice and refine their planning, teaching, and assessment skills in a clinical setting that has been compared to a "teaching hospital."[8] One of the most important advantages for the future teacher is the increased opportunity for feedback from trained mentor teachers in addition to the university supervisor.

Because future teachers are often involved in methods classes while participating in the professional development school, another advantage of PDS programs is the opportunity to apply the learning from methods classes in a "real-life" setting. Future teachers are able to focus planning, teaching, and assessment on actual students and classroom situations that occur as part of their clinical experience. Another important benefit is the opportunity to practice classroom management strategies with diverse students.

Professional development school partnerships offer professional development opportunities for P–12 mentor teachers and administrators who work with future teachers. To be successful, mentor teachers need to receive training in effective communication, supervision strategies, and assessment of student teachers as outlined in the subsequent chapters of this book.

Having PDS interns in the classroom can enhance the professional skills of mentor teachers. For example, as the mentor teacher articulates reasons for the teaching decisions he or she is making to the intern, the mentor engages in critical thinking about his or her teaching practice. As mentors observe interns using innovative teaching strategies, mentors teachers are encouraged to learn about these strategies and apply the strategies in the classroom setting. For P–12 mentor teachers, the opportunity to interact with eager and enthusiastic PDS interns is often exhilarating and may help to reduce stress and burnout. Opportunities to present at professional conferences, to participate in grant writing with university faculty, and to demonstrate effective teaching strategies for future teachers can also enhance the satisfaction and competence of the mentor.

University faculty can also benefit from productive professional development school partnerships. As faculty members interact with mentor and their students, they get an important "reality check" about the increasing diversity and complexity of the P–12 classroom, as well as the high expectations for classroom teachers. When sufficient trust is built with cooperating teachers and administrators, university faculty can use P–12 classrooms to demonstrate strategies for their student teachers, to conduct research and to enhance their professional skills.

Participation in a professional development school partnership can encourage university faculty to return to P–12 classrooms for extended periods of time.[9] When university faculty work in P–12 classrooms, there is more help available for the students in those classrooms and faculty can stay up to date on the issues impacting teachers, students, and schools. Future teachers can benefit from interacting with their professors in actual classroom settings as well.

PDS partnerships can provide opportunities for professional presentations and publications, for grant writing, and for improving professional skills for both P–12 and university faculty members. These opportunities can help the university faculty member to meet requirements for tenure, promotion, and service. One way mentors and university faculty members can collaborate together is by creating electronic textbooks[10] and other curriculum materials for university classes.

P–12 students also benefit from PDS partnerships. P–12 teachers, administrators, and university faculty report improvements in student achievement and attitude when future teachers interact with students as part of the PDS. Other benefits may include future teachers becoming more creative and ambitious in planning lessons and opportunities for action research in the classroom.[11]

Curriculum in a Professional Development School

There are many advantages to increasing the amount of time an intern spends in clinical settings such as a PDS site. A major challenge, however, is to assure that the future teacher acquires the pedagogical knowledge and skills required of beginning teachers. Ideally, methods instructors, mentor teachers, and administrators meet together and determine which experiences and practice opportunities can be found at the PDS site.

One of the challenges in restructuring the methods curriculum is that "we are rebuilding the airplane while it's in flight."[12] Educators at all levels are overworked and overscheduled. Finding time for any new partnership is often difficult. It requires a significant commitment of time to analyze the standards traditionally taught in methods classes and to come up with creative ways to meet these standards and expectations in the *real-world* setting of the professional development school.

Another challenge is the unwillingness of some university instructors to *let go* of some of the content of their classes. Relationships need to be built between university instructors and public school teachers so that the instructors are confident that some of the standards and expectations can be efficiently and appropriately met in the PDS setting.

In analyzing the challenges of faculty-led improvement activities, Robert McClure notes that "if it's not local, it's not real."[13] Restructuring the delivery of the teacher education curriculum means that future teachers will find different curriculum models, teaching strategies, and management styles in different PDS classrooms and schools. It is necessary, therefore, to track each of the standards and expected outcomes and to be open to different ways in which these standards and outcomes may be met in different districts and schools.

Consider, for example, an elementary mathematics methods instructor. This instructor has demonstrated a variety of mathematical strategies and techniques such as hands-on manipulatives, explicit instruction in incorporating the Standards for Mathematical Practice from the Common Core State Standards, small group instruction, differentiated instruction for primary and intermediate interns, and incorporating the use of iPad Apps seamlessly into instruction. Traditionally, mathematics instructors use lecture, discussion, and small group work to teach mathematics to demonstrate these strategies in the university classroom.

Through discussion with public school colleagues and observation in classrooms, the instructor determines that these strategies are used appropriately by mentor teachers at various grade levels in the school. By planning together, the instructor and mentor teachers agree that the future teachers will observe each of these strategies in the PDS setting by observing in various classrooms when the strategies are demonstrated and writing an analysis of how the strategy was demonstrated by the teacher.

This plan requires that the primary teacher who is utilizing iPad apps as a part of a small group mathematics lesson lets the future teachers at the PDS site know when she is planning to teach the lesson. The future teachers come to observe the lesson and complete the required assignment for the university instructor. The upper grade teacher also lets the future teachers know when his students are working in manipulatives to demonstrate the conceptual understanding of adding and subtracting fractions. When interns come to observe, each intern observes one small group in the class. The future teachers meet together after the observation and discuss how the lesson they observed functioned and report their observations to the university instructor.

Restructuring the teacher education curriculum obviously requires a great deal of planning and flexibility. For example, mentor teachers may be hesitant to allow several future teachers to observe in the classroom at one time. It is important to clearly set the guidelines for such observations

Interns are not rating or evaluating the teaching of the mentor—they are analyzing how a specific strategy learned in the university classroom is applied in an actual classroom setting. In some settings, the mentor teacher may be comfortable with the university instructor demonstrating a specific strategy in their classroom while the future teachers observes. This allows the university instructor to model the implementation of a strategy that a mentor teacher may be uncertain about. As the interns observe their university instructor teaching, they may be joined by other classroom teachers at the PDS site who want to observe the strategy. The classroom teachers who observe may want additional instruction and coaching which the university instructor can provide.

Another example of restructuring the curriculum can be found in classroom management class. The classroom management instructor wants future teachers to observe their assigned students using the Classroom Observation Guide (see Table 4.3). After observing and making notes, the intern meets with the mentor teacher who rates the accuracy of the observations. A rubric, developed by the university instructor with input from the mentor teachers, is used by mentors for the rating which is turned in to the university instructor (Table 1.2).

There are several advantages for having the mentor teacher participate in the rating of this assignment. The mentor obviously knows and understands the students in his or her classroom and is in a much better position to rate the accuracy of the future teacher's observations of the students and of the mentor's strategies for working with the students. The intern is required to apply his or her knowledge of students in the PDS classroom. If a particular observation is inaccurate, the university instructor can provide remedial activities as needed.

The most valuable activities for future teachers involve working with individual students, small groups, and the whole class in the PDS setting. Planning assignments with feedback from university instructors and mentor teachers provides valuable feedback to the intern. Working in a PDS classroom helps to assure interns have many opportunities to apply what they are learning by planning and implementing, as they are actually involved in learning the methods content.

Table 1.2. Mentor Teacher Rating for Classroom Management Observations

Rating Scale	Mentor Teacher's Rating of the Intern's Observation Guide*				
	1 strongly agree	2 disagree	3 neutral	4 agree	5 strongly disagree
All required information from the observation guide is completed	1	2	3	4	5
No personally identifiable information about students is included	1	2	3	4	5
Intern describes rules and emergency procedures for the classroom accurately	1	2	3	4	5
Intern describes characteristics of students in the classroom accurately	1	2	3	4	5
Intern describes classroom management strategies used by the mentor teacher accurately	1	2	3	4	5

*Used with Observation Guide, Chapter 4, Table 4.3.

PARTNERSHIPS WITH COMMUNITY COLLEGES

Many teacher education students complete all or part of their general education requirements at a community college. Partnerships between universities and community colleges can provide opportunities to make transfers from community colleges to university teacher education programs more efficient. Publications and web sites can provide assistance in long-term planning. Meetings between community college advisors and university advisors can help each of them to better meet the needs of the teacher education student.[14] With projected teacher shortages and the cost of teacher education tuition, fees, and supplies rising, attracting more teachers into the profession is an important goal. Minority teachers are especially needed.[15] When universities partner with community colleges located in urban areas to share the delivery of the teacher education curriculum on the community college campus site, nontraditional students and future teachers who are place-bound because of family or job needs can complete requirements for teacher education closer to their homes. Future teachers complete the community college courses aligned with the university teacher education program. The students can then continue at the community college site with teacher education courses offered by university faculty.

When universities work together with community colleges, tutorial services for students can be utilized at both sites to assist teacher education students in meeting program requirements. Financial aid and admission procedures can be coordinated so that the student moves from the community college program to the university teacher education program smoothly.[16]

PARTNERSHIPS FOR RECRUITING NEW TEACHER CANDIDATES

Recruiting qualified candidates into teacher education programs is an important challenge. Schools today need to recruit new teachers to replace teachers leaving the profession, to meet shortages in subject matter areas such as math, science, and technology, and to meet the needs of increasingly diverse P–12 student populations. One strategy for recruiting new teachers is to provide high school students with an opportunity to learn about the teaching profession and think about themselves as potential future teachers.

One example of such a partnership is the Kansas Future Teacher Academy, funded by the Kansas legislature. Since the inception of the academy in 1989, over 800 high school students have participated in the academy. The academy meets for five days during the summer on the campus of Emporia State University. Through interaction with guest speakers, including National Teacher Hall of Fame inductees, National State Teachers of the Year, Kansas master teachers, and university faculty, academy participants explore the profession of teaching, match interests and abilities they have to the requirements of teaching, and set goals for the remainder of their high school experience.[17]

Admission to the Kansas Future Teacher Academy is open to public and private high school students. Contacts with high school administrators and counselors help to spread the word about the academy and attract potential attendees. Graduates of the academy are encouraged to recruit younger students at their high schools to attend the academy in future years.

Since attracting minority candidates to teaching is a continuing challenge, another future teacher academy strategy targets middle school students identified by their teachers and counselors to be good candidates for teaching. School districts and universities can work together to bring the identified middle school students to a university campus for a day where the students can interact with each other, with faculty from the school districts, and with university faculty.

SUSTAINING PRODUCTIVE PARTNERSHIPS

Successful partnerships require nurturing in order to sustain the successful outcomes of collaboration. Strategies for sustaining productive partnerships include the following:

Keep in Touch

Continue to schedule regular meetings of the partnership members to discuss problems, make changes, look for ways to enhance the partnership, and celebrate successes.

New Membership

Encourage new staff members to become involved in partnership efforts. New members can help to build on the energy and enthusiasm of the partnership.

Dissemination Opportunities

Look for ways to expand the effectiveness of the partnership through grants, professional publication, and conference presentations.

Rituals and Ceremonies

Creating rituals and ceremonies can enhance the partnership. For example, an open house ceremony can welcome new partners and provide an opportunity for participants from various agencies to get together at the start of a new school year.

Involve Graduates

Teacher education program graduates who become successful teachers are some of the best public relations representatives for partnership efforts. Graduates can be guest speakers for new groups of teacher education students, offering ideas for success and encouragement from those who have "made it." As conference presenters and collaborators on articles, graduates can share personal experiences and insights about the effectiveness of partnership efforts. Additional strategies for sustaining effective partnerships[18] are provided by the state of Washington.

SUMMARY

The challenges facing P–12 schools, community colleges, and universities involved in the preparation of future teachers mandate the need for effective partnerships to make creative and cost-effective use of available resources. Creating effective partnerships requires a commitment of time, energy, and resources for collaboration. Mutual respect and trust must be developed between the stakeholders to assure that the best possible teacher education experience is provided for the future teacher. Increasing the amount of time spent in clinical settings reaffirms the need to train P–12 teachers and administrators in effective supervision practices to maximize the effectiveness of the clinical experience for the future teacher, mentor, university faculty, and the P–12 student.

APPLYING WHAT YOU HAVE LEARNED

Video 1.1

In this video, https://www.youtube.com/watch?v=evs46vOg0gA, you will hear multiple perspectives on the effectiveness of a PDS program. Identify some of the benefits of PDS partnerships which you read about in this chapter as you watch the video. You can check your responses in Appendix 1.

Video 1.2

In this video, https://www.youtube.com/watch?v=QSK4gKaMVY0, you will watch a celebration of twenty years of PDS partners working together. Identify some of the characteristics of effective partnerships which you read about in this chapter as you watch the video. You can check your responses in Appendix 1.

NOTES

1. http://www.edschools.org/pdf/Educating_Teachers_Exec_Summ.pdf
2. http://www.npr.org/sections/ed/2014/06/17/323032745/study-delivers-failing-grades-for-many-programs-training-teachers
3. http://www.edutopia.org/schools-of-education
4. http://www.tc.columbia.edu/centers/pds/charter.htm

5. http://www.ncate.org/ProfessionalDevelopmentSchools/tabid/497/Default.aspx

6. http://napds.org/nine-essentials/

7. Jones, J., Schwerdtfeger, S., Roop, T., and Long, J. (2016). "Trailblazing partnerships: Professional development schools in partnership with Emporia State University." *Journal of the National Association for Professional Development Schools* 9(1), 29–33.

8. Levine, A. (2009). *Educating School Teachers*. Washington, DC: The Education Schools Project, 9.

9. Lyman, L. (2000, February). "A Professor Returns to the Classroom in a Professional Development School." ERIC Resources in Education. Paper presented at the national conference of the Kansas University Professional Development Schools Alliance, Kansas City, Missouri.

10. http://nssa.us/tech_journal/pdf/NSS_Tech_5-2.pdf

11. Hammond, M. (2007, Fall). "Professional Development Schools: Synergy at Its Finest." *School-University Partnerships* 1(2), 6–8.

12. McClure, R. M. (1990). "School Improvement through Colleagueship and Cooperation." In *Cooperative Grouping for Interactive Learning: Students, Teachers, and Administrators*, edited by Lawrence Lyman and Harvey C. Foyle. Washington, DC: National Education Association, 8.

13. McClure, R. M. (1990). "School Improvement through Colleagueship and Cooperation." In *Cooperative Grouping for Interactive Learning: Students, Teachers, and Administrators*, edited by Lawrence Lyman and Harvey C. Foyle. Washington, DC: National Education Association, 8.

14. Mann, L. A. and Lyman, L. (2007, Spring). "Enhancing Public School and University Professional Development School Partnerships: The Community College Link." *School-University Partnerships* 1(1), 81.

15. Kopkowski, C. (2008, January 4). "My Debt, My Life." *NEA Today* 26, 29–33.

16. Mann, L. A. and Lyman, L. (2007, Spring). "Enhancing Public School and University Professional Development School Partnerships: The Community College Link." *School-University Partnerships* 1(1), 81.

17. Jones Institute for Educational Excellence, "Kansas Future Teacher Academy." Retrieved January 8, 2008, from www.emporia.edu/jones/kfta/ index/htm

18. http://www.wa.gov/esd/training/elearning/business/01-06.pdf

Chapter Two

Building Positive Relationships

NURTURING AND SUPPORTIVE RELATIONSHIPS

The mentor teacher provides critical support and guidance for the intern assigned to his or her class. The mentor helps to ensure a positive clinical experience by developing a nurturing professional relationship, supervising the intern's teaching, and evaluating progress. Table 2.1 represents the skills needed by the mentor teacher in order to assist an intern's growth professionally and provide a supportive atmosphere.

It is important to remember that the mentor provides opportunities for the intern to be successful during the internship experience. Even the most caring and competent teacher cannot guarantee the success of an intern in a specific classroom setting. Knowledge, skills, and dispositions that the intern brings to the internship often determine the degree of success he or she will experience. Attitude, maturity, and work ethic will also affect the quality of the intern's experience. These factors are usually beyond the control of the mentor teacher. Examples of the knowledge, skills, and dispositions[1] required of successful interns can be found in the PDS Policy and Procedures Book from Emporia State University (pages 9, 10, and 11).

Table 2.1. Mentor Teacher Skills

Modeling and Explaining	*Planning Skills*	*Supervision Skills*
Good teaching practices	Instructional planning	Collecting data
Positive, professional attitude	Sequencing	Reinforcing
Communication skills	Orientation	Clarifying
Building trust		Brainstorming
Positive regard		Remediating

INITIAL CONTACT WITH THE PROSPECTIVE INTERN

Interview

A positive relationship can begin when the mentor teacher interviews the prospective intern prior to being accepted for placement in the mentor's classroom. An interview of twenty to thirty minutes lets a mentor become acquainted with the intern and may identify potential problems or conflicts that need to be addressed before a placement is finalized. Interviews can assist both the mentor and intern in determining if the placement is appropriate. A list of possible interview questions is provided in Table 2.2.

When meeting an intern for the first time, the mentor needs to realize that many interns will be nervous and might appear to lack confidence.[2] It is important to remember during an initial interview that the intern is at an early stage of his or her professional development and will usually gain confidence as he or she becomes familiar with the mentor and the students.

A potential problem for some mentor teachers is the comparison of the prospective intern with another, whom the mentor supervised previously. Such comparisons are almost always unfair to both the previous intern and the prospective intern. Mentors need to be aware of the human tendency to make such comparisons and be careful to judge each prospective intern on his or her own merits. A helpful overview of the interview process[3] is provided by Fresno State University.

Table 2.2. Interview Questions for Prospective Interns

These questions were adapted from a list created by professional development school coordinators from Emporia State University and mentor teachers and principals from Professional Development Schools in the Emporia (Kansas) and Olathe (Kansas) Public Schools.

Tell me about yourself.
Why do you want to be a teacher?
Why are you interested in an internship at this grade level? Why are you interested in an internship at this school?
What kinds of experiences have you had with children? Have you had experiences with culturally diverse groups of students?
Tell me about a student with whom you have worked and who was a real challenge for you.
What is your philosophy of teaching?
As a student, what subjects do you like best and why?
What are your strengths?
Tell me about a teacher who had a strong positive influence on you.

BUILDING A POSITIVE RELATIONSHIP

The professional relationship between the intern and the mentor is crucial to the intern's success.[4] A positive, professional relationship can help make the intern feel comfortable in the classroom. Additionally, when interns feel accepted, they are more likely to demonstrate positive attitudes toward students and adults in the school, and be more productive and successful in teaching. When a positive and professional relationship is established, interns are usually more receptive to feedback and suggestions for improvement.

Building a positive and professional relationship with an intern requires that the mentor be a competent professional who models good teaching practices and is capable of and willing to explain the reasons for teaching decisions. A mentor's positive, professional attitude toward teaching, students, colleagues, and parents is a crucial model for the intern's own development of appropriate attitudes and behaviors.

The mentor teacher must communicate positively and effectively so that necessary information about the teaching context is communicated. Expectations for planning, teaching, assessment, and classroom management need to be clearly communicated to the intern and modeled by the mentor consistently. Feedback provided to the intern must be constructive and helpful. Building trust with the intern will evolve from this open and positive communication approach.

As the instructional leader in the classroom, the mentor is responsible for providing guidance, feedback, and support to the intern. As Kouzes and Posner point out, "Strategies, tactics, skills, and practices are empty unless we understand the fundamental human aspirations that connect leaders and their constituents."[5]

PREREQUISITE MENTOR TEACHER SKILLS AND ATTITUDES

To be effective, a mentor must first be a competent teacher in the classroom and must model behaviors and attitudes expected of good teachers. One of the most critical areas of a mentor's performance in the classroom is the ability to establish and maintain a positive learning environment for all students. If this component of effective teaching is lacking, the intern will almost certainly be better served in another classroom. The placement of an intern is not to support or assist a mediocre or poor teacher. As mentor teacher placements are considered, it is essential that the most dedicated and best teachers be given first priority. Edutopia[6] provides additional qualities of effective teachers.

Not all educators who are effective teachers of K–12 students are equally as effective working with interns. Identifying and explaining the rationale for teaching decisions are important skills for mentor teachers. Utilizing these skills requires a mentor to be confident in making teaching decisions and not be threatened when questioned about these decisions by an intern. Thinking about the reasons why a teaching decision was made and articulating those reasons is a metacognitive process that provides professional growth for the mentor a well as the intern.[7]

Mentor teachers need to be mature professionals who model effective teaching and interpersonal skills. Three domains[8] in which teachers need to demonstrate maturity are professional, personal, and process.

A mentor teacher needs to be willing to accept input from the intern about his or her observations of the teaching and learning processes occurring in the classroom. One of the most rewarding aspects of working with an intern is having another set of eyes viewing the students in the classroom. Like all good teachers, mentors must make use of all available input and ideas to improve their interactions with students. Because teachers are required to make so many decisions each day, some decisions could be clarified and improved upon thorough reflection and discussion with an intern.[9]

Finally, mentor teachers must be willing to share their classrooms and students with another professional. Some competent classroom teachers are simply not comfortable in relinquishing control of their students to another teacher. If this is so, the intern and the students in the classroom may sense this discomfort and the intern's experience is less likely to be successful.

Insisting that the intern use only strategies and methods of teaching used by the mentor may be another indication of unwillingness to relinquish control. Problems in sharing the classroom and students are sometimes evidenced if the mentor teacher feels the need to publicly correct the intern while he is teaching. Although public suggestions may be necessary at time, if used inappropriately such corrections will undermine the credibility of the intern. If an intern is corrected publicly and inappropriately, students may stop listening to the intern. The intern may lose confidence and trust in the mentor teacher.

As the intern becomes more skilled, he or she will benefit from more freedom. Allowing the competent intern to try different strategies and methods usually benefits both the intern and the students in the classroom. Additional discussion of the importance of the mentor teacher role and characteristics of effective mentor teachers can be found in articles from ASCD[10] and *Education Week*.[11]

SKILLS AND PRACTICES THAT PROMOTE POSITIVE RELATIONSHIPS

Positive, Professional Attitude

Mentors must demonstrate a positive and professional attitude toward teaching, students, parents, and colleagues when working with an intern. A myriad of challenges face every classroom teacher, but cynicism and negative approaches are discouraging and draining for all professionals. A mentor teacher with a negative attitude can be debilitating to even the most enthusiastic beginning teacher. Mentors who view teaching as an exciting and rewarding profession are the best models for future teachers. These mentors are characterized by their willingness to try new ideas and methods with all students. Their classrooms are positive learning environments[12] where learners are actively engaged in appropriate experiences.

Good mentors demonstrate positive relationships[13] with students, and classroom management is accomplished while protecting the dignity of the students. Mentors should demonstrate equity in dealing with students and be regarded by students as fair and consistent.

High expectations[14] for the learning and success of all students are a hallmark of a good mentor's classrooms. This standard should be modeled in practice by the mentor, expected of the students, and required of the intern. These three elements will improve the likelihood of the intern's success.

The mentor teacher should consistently model professionalism when dealing with students, colleagues, administrators, and parents. For example, the mentors need to avoid sharing negative feelings and attitudes toward another teacher, principal, student, or parent. This may be difficult in schools where gossip in the faculty lounge is the norm, but the mentor must set the tone for professional behavior to help overcome negative models that may be observed by an intern.

Sharing confidential information about colleagues, parents, or administrators must be done only in the context of a "need to know" basis. If, in the judgment of the mentor, an intern needs to be aware of information that could be considered confidential to assist him or her in teaching more effectively, the mentor may need to discuss this information.

Communication Skills

The ideal intern experience is characterized by many opportunities to share ideas and information, both formally and informally. Effective communication requires the mentor to demonstrate skills of listening, sharing information, and giving feedback.

Listening effectively[15] to others is a vital communication skill. Covey[16] states, "If I were to summarize in one sentence the single most important principle I have learned in the field of interpersonal relations, it would be this: Seek first to understand, then to be understood."[17] Effective listening can help the mentor understand the points of view, the educational decision-making processes, and the concerns of the intern

Effective listening takes time. The mentor teacher must find time in an already busy and overcrowded schedule to meet with the intern on a regular basis. During these meetings, a mentor should make the effort to communicate effectively. By putting other tasks aside and taking the time to listen, the mentor lets the intern know that providing feedback and sharing ideas are important. Demonstrating active listening skills while communicating with the intern will improve interpersonal relations and foster an environment of trust.

Effective listeners use several techniques to accomplish goals, such as making comments, asking questions to draw the speaker out, and attempting to gather further information. They also use body language, including eye contact, posture, and positive facial expressions. Finally, asking questions to clarify the point of view of the intern is an important strategy for effective communication.

Positive communication with the intern can be enhanced through the use of affirmation statements. These statements can be used to encourage an intern encountering difficulties with certain aspects of teaching such as classroom management or student relations. Affirmation statements can also be used to remind an intern of beliefs or ideals. For example, encourage the mentor by affirming that his or her effort and persistence will promote student success.

Another use for the affirmation statement is to indicate that the mentor teacher has faith in the intern's ability to solve a problem. For example, the mentor could assure the intern that he or she has the skills to plan well-organized lessons. The mentor affirms that planning effective lessons will take time but improved student learning and better classroom management will result. Affirmation statements that reflect the mentor's true attitudes and are delivered without sarcasm or hidden agendas can facilitate positive communication, even in potentially negative situations.

Effective Feedback

One of the most important functions of the mentor teacher is to provide feedback about the intern's planning, teaching, assessment, and classroom management. Effective feedback has five characteristics: amount, specificity, frequency, timing, and relevancy.

Amount

The amount of feedback given to an intern needs to be appropriate. Too much feedback can confuse an intern and be difficult for the intern to apply. Too little feedback may inhibit the professional growth of the intern. In formative conferences with an intern, concentrating on one or two specific areas to maintain, change, or improve instruction is advisable. Focusing on only one or two key themes will give the mentor an opportunity to determine if the intern is able to apply the feedback and recommendations.

Specificity

Feedback that includes specific examples from the intern's daily teaching can enhance understanding and performance. Regular, specific feedback can improve an intern's ability to implement recommendations for improvement and, therefore, impact the learning of students in a positive manner. Specific and clearly defined recommendations benefit the intern by clarifying performance expectations. Suggestions for action need to focus upon improving and modifying instructional strategies.

Frequency

Frequency refers to how often feedback is provided. Usually, shorter, more frequent conferences with the intern are preferable. Short conferences held more frequently are usually more effective. Early in the experience feedback will be more frequent as expectations are being clarified, usually daily, and sometimes hourly. More frequent feedback also occurs if the intern is not performing as expected. Throughout the internship, frequent conferences and feedback are essential to the success.

Timing

Feedback should be timed so that it can be useful to the student. Feedback is usually most effective when the intern has opportunities to apply the recommendations soon after the feedback is provided. Mentors should be sensitive to the timing of feedback after a stressful experience. Positive reinforcement and specific suggestions for changes provided as soon as possible after teaching can help an intern succeed.

Relevancy

Useful feedback will be relevant and specific. Relevant feedback deals with issues that impact student learning during the lesson. For example, if two students are off task and the mentor helps the intern identify that behavior through questions or guided discussion, it can help the intern be aware of such behavior and address it appropriately in future lessons. Useful suggestions from the mentor can help the intern gain confidence and make needed improvements. As interns demonstrate increased skills, mentors can encourage interns to brainstorm ideas and solutions as well.

Effective communication is the by-product of the mentor's genuine desire to understand the perspective and attitudes of the intern as well as the reasons for his or her teaching decisions. Taking the time to communicate effectively[18] is a very important element in the process of building trust with the intern.

Building Trust with the Intern

Developing a climate of trust[19] in the mentor and intern relationship is necessary for effective supervision to take place.[20] According to Lyman et al., teachers in general have legitimate concerns about the process of assessing their competence.[21] When trust between intern and mentor[22] is present, the intern is more likely to be successful.

Two kinds of trust are important: interpersonal and procedural trust. Interpersonal trust is created when the intern feels that difficult issues with the mentor can be discussed without having the information used negatively or communicated inappropriately to a third party. For example, the intern may confide to the mentor teacher that the workload is causing stress. Trust would be diminished considerably if the mentor were to share this information with colleagues in the teachers' lounge.

Interpersonal trust is enhanced when an intern feels that personal feelings and property are treated with respect and dignity. With so much to do, it is easy for a mentor to inadvertently disregard an intern's feelings with an unintended remark. When interpersonal trust is present, both parties feel comfortable sharing concerns and resolving problems quickly.

It is also important that the intern has a physical space within the classroom that is professional, private, and secure and where professional and personal items can be stored. Both the students in the classroom and the mentor need to respect this personal space.

Procedural trust is built when the intern knows that the mentor clearly understands and follows the expectations and policies related to the internship. An intern has the right to expect the mentor and the university supervisor to abide by rules and regulations set forth in university documents and procedure manuals. A common concern occurs when the intern is asked to substitute for the mentor when the mentor is absent from the classroom. This request almost always violates the university's policy for the clinical experience and may violate district policy and state law.[23]

Procedural trust is enhanced when the mentor teacher and university supervisor adhere to assessments and schedules required by the university. For example, if a weekly conference between the mentor and intern is indicated by university policy, the mentor should make such a conference a priority, even if time considerations limit the length of such a conference.

University supervisors should be careful to make the number of visits to the classroom as directed by the university, observe the intern for the prescribed length of time, and utilize the appropriate forms for giving formative and summative feedback during each visit.

Lyman, Morehead, and Foyle have identified a number of additional factors that build teacher trust. These factors include positive tone, clear expectations, useful feedback, and concern for the intern.[24]

Positive tone[25] during interactions with interns results from the mentor focusing on the intern's strengths and the appropriate behaviors and attitudes the intern demonstrates. It is important for the intern to have a clear understanding of what he or she is doing well in the classroom so that these skills can be applied in future lessons, job interviews, and in their own classrooms. It is important that the intern know what the teacher expects and that the teacher provides information needed about the students that is needed for the intern to be successful.

Mentors need to make clear what their expectations[26] for effective teaching and classroom management are, as well as any *pet peeves* the mentor may have. A mentor and intern relationship can turn sour when expectations are not clarified. For example, a particular way to grade, not following classroom procedures, or not being punctual can cause a mentor to become irritated with an intern. Below is a list of desired behaviors that may help the mentor clarify his or her expectations for an intern.

Communicating Concern and Positive Regard

Concern for the intern is expressed by the mentor in the way in which the mentor communicates with the intern and builds trust. Concern for the intern is demonstrated by providing information about the school culture, environment, and expectations. Specific information about the context of the school and classroom in which the intern will be working is needed. Taking time to orient the intern to school personnel, locations of pertinent offices, school procedures, and other relevant information can help an intern to feel at ease and may avoid problems.

As indicated earlier, useful feedback builds trust and also demonstrates concern for the success and growth of the intern. Feedback that recognizes unique strengths and qualities lets the intern know he or she is valued and appreciated by the mentor. By identifying strengths and discussing them, a mentor will encourage productivity and help to build trust. Focusing on teaching behaviors rather than on personal traits when giving feedback provides the intern with the best opportunity to make positive changes that impact student learning.

Mentor teachers can also demonstrate their support for an intern by communicating positive regard. As professionals, interns need to feel that their efforts are appreciated[27] and that they are making progress toward their goals. The mentor can communicate positive regard and build confidence by using the following strategies.

Showing consideration
   Goal: For the mentor to demonstrate a caring approach.
   "I know you weren't feeling well yesterday. Are you feeling better today?"
   "How are you doing in your evening class?"
   "I heard you had a great interview. Congratulations."

Showing appreciation
   Goal: For the mentor to recognize and value effort.
   "Thanks for all your hard work on that bulletin board. It looks great."
   "I appreciate the way you have been working with Dudley. His attitude is improving."
   "It's such a help to have you here."

Sharing positive feedback
   Goal: For the mentor to share positive feedback from others.
   "The substitute yesterday said you did a great job with the class."
   "The principal told me how well you handled the disruption on the playground today."
   "Amy's mother told me how pleased she was with the creative writing lessons you are teaching."

Sharing positive feedback about teaching behaviors
   Goal: For the mentor to reinforce effective teaching behaviors
   "The class scores on that test were very impressive."
   "You handled that student's incorrect answer expertly."
   "Every student had a chance to participate successfully this morning."

SUMMARY

Developing positive mentor and intern relationships requires effort on the part of both the mentor and the intern. The mentor's effort is usually rewarded by the positive environment and productivity that result from

Table 2.3. Mentor Teacher Checklist for Assessing Skills in Developing Positive Relationships with Interns

Proficient	Competent	Needs Work
I model appropriate teaching behaviors and strategies.		
I am able to explain the reasons for teaching decisions I make.		
I have a positive, professional attitude in dealing with students, colleagues, and parents.		
I demonstrate effective communication skills.		
I make expectations clear to the intern.		
I can build intern trust.		
I demonstrate positive regard for the intern.		
I am willing to share my classroom and students with another professional.		
I am willing to invest the time and effort it takes to develop positive relationships with my intern.		

positive relationships. Interns who work with mentors who take time to develop positive relationships will find their experience less stressful and more rewarding. A checklist for the mentor teacher to use in assessing his or her skills and practices for developing positive relationships with an intern is found in Table 2.3.

APPLYING WHAT YOU HAVE LEARNED

Video 2.1

In this video, https://youtu.be/zpQmP8r5DIs, you will observe a conference between a mentor teacher and an intern focusing on a relationship problem perceived by the mentor teacher. Make a list of positive examples of the concepts from this chapter that you see the mentor modeling in the conference. You can check your list in Appendix 1.

Video 2.2

In this video, https://youtu.be/74RtFeKqAxg, you will observe a conference between a mentor teacher and an intern about a problem that the intern is having in relating to one of the students in the class. Make a list of positive examples from this chapter that you see the mentor modeling in the conference. You can check your list in Appendix 1.

NOTES

1. https://www.emporia.edu/dotAsset/f7239bd6-c2ad-4371-9861-b8b09e1b303c.pdf
2. Caruso, J. J. (2000, January). "Cooperating Teacher and Student Teacher Phases of Development." *Young Children* 55(1), 75–81.
3. http://fresnostate.edu/kremen/applications/msreqs.html
4. Silva, D. Y. (2000). "Triad Journaling as a Tool for Reconceptualizing Supervision in the Professional Development School." Proceedings from American Educational Research Association, New Orleans, 1–17.
5. Kouzes, J. M. and Posner, B. Z. (1993). *Credibility: How Leaders Gain and Lose It, Why People Demand It.* San Francisco: Jossey-Bass, 1.
6. http://www.edutopia.org/discussion/11-habits-effective-teacher
7. Ganser, T. (1997). "The Contribution of Service as a Cooperating Teacher and Mentor Teacher to the Professional Development of Teachers." Proceedings from American Educational Research Association, Chicago, 1–62.
8. http://jte.sagepub.com/content/36/4/55.extract
9. Ganser, T. (1997, March). "The Contribution of Service as a Cooperating Teacher and Mentor Teacher to the Professional Development of Teachers." Proceedings from the American Educational Research Association, Chicago, 1–62.
10. http://www.ascd.org/publications/educational-leadership/may99/vol56/num08/The-Good-Mentor.aspx
11. http://www.edweek.org/tm/articles/2014/09/30/ctq_long_mentor.html
12. http://www.edutopia.org/discussion/32-strategies-building-positive-learning-environment
13. http://www.nea.org/tools/29469.htm
14. http://www.middleweb.com/24030/do-we-really-have-high-expectations/
15. http://www.skillsyouneed.com/ips/listening-types.html
16. http://www.behavior-change.net/covey-5-seek-first-to-understand-then-to-be-understood/
17. Covey, S. R. (1989). *The 7 Habits of Highly Effective People.* New York: Simon and Schuster, 235–260.
18. http://lifehacker.com/top-10-ways-to-improve-your-communication-skills-1590488550
19. http://greatergood.berkeley.edu/article/item/how_to_build_trust_in_schools
20. Lyman, L. and Foyle, H. C. (1990). *Cooperative Groupings for Interactive Learning: Students, Teachers, and Administrators.* Washington, DC: National Education Association, 59–60.
21. Lyman, L., Wilson, A. P., Garhart, C. K., Heim, M. O., and Winn, W. O. (1987). *Clinical Instruction and Supervision for Accountability.* Dubuque, Iowa: Kendall/Hunt, 106.
22. http://blogs.maryville.edu/shausfather/vita/ethics-pds/
23. Slick, S. K. (1998, September–October). "A University Supervisor Negotiates Territory and Status." *Journal of Teacher Education* 49(4), 306–315.
24. Lyman, L., Morehead, M. A., and Foyle, H. C. (1989, Winter). "Building Teacher Trust in Supervision and Evaluation." *Illinois School Research and Development* 25(2), 55–59.

25. https://blog.bufferapp.com/why-positive-encouragement-works-better-than-criticism-according-to-science

26. http://www.inc.com/guides/2010/08/how-to-communicate-employee-expectations-effectively.html

27. http://www.littlethingsmatter.com/blog/2010/02/24/the-power-of-showing-your-appreciation/

Chapter Three

Student Teaching Program Assessment and Accountability

The clinical experiences that a future teacher is involved in during his or her teacher preparation program are crucial to helping the future teacher acquire, practice, and enhance the skills needed to be successful in the classroom. The university must assure that a comprehensive program of assessment determines the future teacher's readiness to participate in each phase of the preparation program.

Assessment[1] during the clinical experiences, which ideally is completed in a Professional Development School (PDS) setting, provides the most important source of information about the future teacher's progress. Active involvement of mentor teachers in the assessment process improves the quantity and quality of feedback the future teacher receives, if mentors and university supervisor are well trained in their roles.

Since clinical field experiences are so important to the success of the future teacher, regular assessment of the student teaching program[2] needs to occur to assure that the program is effective and accountable. Feedback from a variety of stakeholders, including students in the program, graduates of the program, mentor teachers, and employers of graduates of the program, needs to be analyzed on a systematic basis.

ROLE OF UNIVERSITY FACULTY

University faculty have the primary responsibility for assuring that future teachers meet the requirements of the teacher education program, appropriate subject matter standards, and state licensure standards. A variety of assessment tools,[3] emphasizing authentic, performance-based assessment, are necessary to document that future teachers have demonstrated mastery of requirements.

Record keeping, which assures that each candidate has met the requirements, can be time-consuming and personnel-intensive. However, having comprehensive data[4] on each participant in the program is crucial for the accountability of the program and to meet accreditation and legal requirements.

Faculty who work with teacher candidates before they enter a teacher education program can provide important input about the knowledge, skills, and dispositions of students. Soliciting information from faculty members who teach courses required before admission to the program can assist the admissions committee in making appropriate decisions. A concern form, provided for the use of faculty, is a helpful tool in encouraging feedback from faculty who may have useful information from contact with students in their classes.

Since many future teachers complete some or all of their general education requirements at a community college, communication with community college instructors is also important. Community college partnerships, as discussed earlier, can provide opportunities for dialogue about future teachers. In the absence of such partnership agreements, regular meetings with instructors from community colleges with high numbers of transfer students to the university can be very helpful in making sure future teachers are ready for the teacher education program.

Teacher education and liberal arts faculty who work with future teachers in methods classes have a key role in assessment. Through contacts with future teachers, observation of interpersonal skills during class, conferences outside of class, and evaluation of course assignments, methods instructors gain vital insights about the skills of future teachers.

Regular meetings with methods teachers to discuss the progress of students in their classes provide important opportunities for formative assessment of the progress of candidates. Midterm meetings can identify students who are struggling in one or more classes. If a student is having difficulty in several classes and common problems or concerns are noted, the methods faculty may choose to meet with the candidate and discuss their concerns. Because meeting with a group of instructors can be intimidating, one or two instructors from the group may meet with students instead of a large group of faculty.

At the conclusion of the semester when methods classes are taken, it is again useful to have the methods instructors meet to discuss the summative assessments of students in the program. It is essential to have university supervisors who will be working with the students in clinical settings and appropriate representatives from the academic department and student teaching office attend meetings. They can identify potential concerns or problems with students they will be working with.

When problems and concerns have been identified during methods classes, a useful strategy is for the student teaching director, department chair, or other designee to meet with the future teacher and prepare a contract specifying the conditions for successful participation in the clinical experience. If punctuality and attendance have been problems in the methods classes, for example, the contract may specify a maximum number of absences or late arrivals permitted during the clinical experience. The contract may require the future teacher to contact the university supervisor in the event of any absence, late arrival, or early departure so that any potential problems in the clinical experience can be dealt with proactively.

During the clinical experiences, the university supervisor or supervisors gather data about the performance of future teachers through regular observations, contacts with the intern, and contacts with the mentor teachers. If both an academic and an education supervisor are assigned to an intern, it is important that they communicate together. If concerns about the knowledge, skills, or dispositions of the intern occur during the clinical experiences, a contract may be created to specify the criteria for successful completion of the clinical experience.

Alignment of schedules for observing the intern is one issue that academic and education supervisors can discuss. It is seldom helpful, for example, for two supervisors to visit the intern on the same day, and this issue can be avoided by communication. More importantly, if problems or concerns are noted in the performance of the intern, the supervisors can work together to provide the remediation needed to assist the intern.

THE ROLE OF THE MENTOR TEACHER

The mentor teacher has the best opportunity to assess the student teaching intern and provide helpful feedback because they are in daily contact. The mentor also has in-depth understanding of the academic, social, and behavioral needs of the students in his or her class that the university supervisor will not have.

Because mentor teachers have multiple roles, it is sometimes difficult for the mentor to find the time needed to provide feedback to the intern. Structuring the assessments in the student teaching program so that a weekly conference with the mentor teacher and the intern is required helps to assure that regular feedback is provided to the intern and that the progress of the intern is documented.

An important responsibility of the mentor teacher is to assess the quality of the planning, implementation, and assessment of instruction by the intern. Classroom management, organization, time management, and relationships with students are also important areas for the mentor teacher to assess. Requiring at least one weekly formative assessment encourages the mentor teacher and intern to meet regularly to discuss areas of strength and areas for growth in these important areas of teaching.

Mentor teachers can also provide helpful feedback about the student teaching program and the quality of preparation of the future teachers they work with. It is important to involve mentor teachers when discussing changes in the structure, classes, or assessments for the teacher education program, as their input can be invaluable.

THE ROLE OF THE BUILDING PRINCIPAL

Like mentor teachers, building principals have multiple roles to fulfill that can limit their availability to work with interns. Building principals can serve as another source of feedback to interns about their performance when invited to observe in the classroom and their schedules permit them to do so. As trained observers, principals can add to the information interns have about their teaching and provide additional suggestions for professional growth.

One of the advantages of working with interns in a PDS setting is the opportunity for principals to observe candidates for potential teaching positions in the school or district. Interacting with interns in classroom settings can help the administrator assess the suitability of the future teacher for the school or for other positions in the school district. Interns who are a good match for a school or district can be identified early and hired before they take positions elsewhere.

TRAINING FOR MENTOR TEACHERS AND UNIVERSITY SUPERVISORS

Working successfully with interns requires that both mentor teachers and university supervisors have specific training. The ability to build a positive relationship with the intern, to help to plan and sequence the student teaching experience appropriately, and to supervise the intern, giving appropriate feedback and dealing with problems and concerns, are discussed in subsequent chapters of this book. Specific suggestions for developing effective training programs for mentor teachers and university supervisors can be found in the final chapter of this book.

It is the responsibility of the university to assure that those who work with future teachers have the training needed to do so effectively. University supervisors should be required to participate in a training program that provides them with information about the program, especially requirements for assessments. Opportunities to practice the required skills for successful supervision are another important attribute of a successful training program. It cannot be assumed that a faculty member who is knowledgeable in his or her discipline automatically has the skills needed to supervise interns effectively.

Appropriate training and ongoing support for mentor teachers is also necessary.[5] As with the university supervisor, the training should focus on the requirements of the program and the skills needed for successful supervision of the intern. Ideally, successful completion of the training program would be required before an intern would be assigned to a mentor teacher.

Incentives are needed to encourage busy university supervisors and mentor teachers to participate in training. For the university supervisor, a stipend for travel may be appreciated. Stipends may also encourage participation by mentor teachers. Providing university credit for mentor teachers participating in the training program may also serve as an inducement to participate in training.

Designing training programs to assure that university supervisors and mentor teachers have the skills needed to work effectively with interns requires an investment of both time and money. Faculty conducting the training will require compensation or load credit, in addition to the stipends paid for those attending the training sessions. However, the importance of assuring that every university supervisor and mentor teacher has been specifically trained for their roles as supervisors cannot be overstated.

Interns can provide valuable feedback about the effectiveness of the mentor teacher[6] and the university supervisor.[7] It is also useful to get feedback from mentor teachers and building principals about the effectiveness of the university supervisor who works with their school site.

THE IMPORTANCE OF DISPOSITIONS

Since 2002, the National Council for Accreditation of Teacher Education has mandated that accredited teacher education programs identify and assess dispositions for successful teaching[8] for future teachers. These dispositions are required as a part of the conceptual framework of the teacher education unit.[9]

Observing and assessing dispositions in future teachers needs to begin in general education classes. As stated earlier, general education faculty at the teacher education university and in community colleges can provide important information for assessment of the expected dispositions[10] before the candidate is admitted to teacher education.

Communication about dispositions between mentor teachers and university faculty is especially important because mentor teachers can have an important influence on the way interns develop and demonstrate desired dispositions.

Mentor teachers and university faculty members need to work together to assure that the dispositions identified for assessment are appropriate and that the methods for assessing the dispositions are effective.[11]

Example of Dispositions for Teacher Education Candidates

1. Professionalism and ethical standards.
2. Respect for cultural and individual differences by providing equitable learning opportunities for all students.
3. A willingness to think critically about content, curriculum planning, teaching and learning pedagogy, innovative technology, and assessment.
4. The belief that educating children and adults requires the integration of multiple kinds of knowledge.
5. A desire to analyze concepts, evaluate clinical practices, experiment, and initiate innovative practices as needed.
6. A commitment to life-long learning by participating in professional organizations and by keeping current with research in their field.
7. A commitment to challenge all students to learn and to help every child to succeed.
8. An awareness of the larger social contexts within which learning occurs.
9. A commitment to self-reflection to recognize in all students human physical, cognitive, social, and emotional development.
10. A belief that curriculum planning and teaching practices must be meaningful, engaging, and adapted to the needs of diverse learners.
11. A desire to collaborate with colleagues, parents and community members, and other educators to improve student learning.
12. A willingness to learn from other professionals in the field.

Source: The Teachers College, Emporia State University[12]

Dispositions should be a part of the assessment process used to determine whether future teachers are sufficiently prepared to be effective in their own classrooms. As with other assessments used in the teacher education program, disposition assessments should be aligned with the Conceptual Framework of the institution.

SELF-ASSESSMENT

As the intern begins working with students, part of the assessment of his or her work needs to include appropriate self-assessment. Interns must have the capability and desire to assess their knowledge, skills, dispositions,[13] and teaching performance[14] on an ongoing basis.

Using data from planning, teaching, and student assessment, future teachers need to be able to identify what is going well and to identify and implement appropriate changes as needed.

An important part of self-assessment is to help the intern identify areas of needed improvement and to develop strategies for working toward those improvements. In their own classrooms, future teachers will need to be proactive, not waiting for feedback to monitor and adjust their teaching.

Future teachers also need to be able to identify specific strengths they have in the classroom. Often, the solution to an instructional problem can be found by looking at what the intern does well and capitalizing on these strengths.

In the supervisory process outlined in chapter 4 of this book, conferences with the intern are at first primarily planned and conducted by mentor teachers and university supervisors. As an intern's clinical experiences progress, one of the measures of the professional growth of the intern is his or her ability to analyze teaching performance accurately with progressively less assistance from supervisors.

TEACHER WORK SAMPLES

Teacher work samples can provide evidence of the intern's ability to plan, teach, and assess while meeting expected standards. A teacher work sample can be defined as "an exhibit of teaching performance that provides direct evidence" of the intern's competence in instructional planning, implementation, and assessment.[15]

The Renaissance Group of teacher education colleges has developed a model for teacher work samples[16] that requires the intern to provide evidence of accountability for the learning of the students he or she is working with. In the Renaissance Teacher Work Sample model, teaching performance standards with indicators are specified. Prompts, teaching tasks, and rubrics are provided to assist the intern as he or she develops the teacher work sample. A scoring rubric for each task is provided. The outcomes of the teacher work sample must be aligned with state or local standards, and the intern must analyze the student learning that took place by comparing pretest and posttest data from the students in the class he or she is teaching.

As with any assessment, the factors assessed by teacher work samples should be aligned with other assessments and the Conceptual Framework of the institution. Factors which may be found in a teacher work sample include

1. contextual information;
2. goals and learning outcomes;
3. instructional design and implementation, integration skills;
4. classroom learning environment, classroom management, motivation;

5. analysis of assessment procedures and impact on student learning; and
6. reflection and self-evaluation.

Source: Black Hills State University[17]

Training on the teacher work sample process is a necessary part of the training provided to mentor teachers and university supervisors. Professionals working with interns need to be able to provide appropriate assistance to interns without helping them too much.

Evaluators of the teacher work samples need additional training to be able to assess the teacher work sample fairly and to assure inter-rater reliability. As with training for supervision, teacher work sample training requires a willingness to expend time and funding. The teacher work sample provides important performance-based evidence of the intern's impact on student learning that justifies the necessary time and expense.

ACCOUNTABILITY THROUGH ASSESSMENT

Calls for teacher education programs to be more accountable for the performance of future teachers are intensifying.[18] One of the ways teacher education programs can demonstrate their effectiveness is through the assessment data collected during the preparation of future teachers.

Most teacher education programs collect a great deal of assessment data[19] about their students. It is important to analyze that data cooperatively, with other stakeholders as well as members of the university staff, to identify strengths and weaknesses of the teacher education program and to assure that a meaningful experience is provided for all candidates.

It is also important that assessments be aligned with the conceptual framework of the college. In the student teaching program, for example, assessment forms need to reflect the specific competencies and skills expected of the intern. Ideally, multiple assessments of program standards, at various stages of the teacher education program, will demonstrate the achievement of future teachers.

Mentor teachers and university supervisors as well as interns can provide important feedback about the usefulness of student teaching assessment forms. Terminology, format, or rating scales may be confusing or unclear. With regular feedback from supervisors and candidates, the quality of the feedback provided to the intern can be assured.

ACCOUNTABILITY THROUGH SHARED GOVERNANCE

Sharing the responsibility for governance, oversight, and assessment of teacher education can be facilitated by creating shared governance[20] procedures. For example, P–12 teachers and administrators may meet on a regular basis with university teachers and administrators to discuss the progress of shared teacher education efforts. Education faculty members and administrators may meet on a regular basis with their liberal arts and sciences colleagues to discuss the curriculum and assessment of the teacher education curriculum.

When a large number of teacher education students are placed in a school district as freshman and sophomore observers and tutors, as juniors working with small groups of students under university faculty supervision, and as seniors working as interns, a *teacher council* may be created with membership from P–12 school mentor teachers and administrators and university teachers and administrators. Goals of such a council can include coordination of dates for beginning and ending placement experiences, discussion of assessments, identification of concerns and problems, and celebration of successful efforts in preparing future teachers.

To coordinate the efforts of liberal arts and science faculty and education faculty working with teacher education students, a *teacher education council* may be useful. Each department involved in the preparation of future teachers has representation on the council. Among the responsibilities of the council are providing input about proposed teacher education curricular changes, analyzing admission requirements and assessments of teacher education students, and celebrating successful efforts in preparing future teachers.

As partnerships with community colleges are developed, shared governance procedures are also useful. Representatives from each of the stakeholder groups involved in the partnership should meet together on a regular basis to assure that the goals of the partnership are being met.

ACCOUNTABILITY THROUGH EVALUATION

An important part of the assessment of the student teaching program comes from stakeholders in the program. Feedback from instructors, mentor teachers, and university supervisors should be systematically collected and analyzed to determine the strengths and needs of the program. Feedback from interns currently enrolled in the program is extremely useful as well. While collecting and analyzing data from stakeholders is time-consuming, the quality of the student teaching program depends on this feedback.

Feedback from graduates of the teacher education program and from administrators who have employed graduates as teachers is another source of valuable evidence of the effectiveness of the teacher education program. When PDS models are utilized, the feedback from employers is ongoing as schools and districts participating in professional development school programs often hire graduates to teach in their own schools.

One of the measures of effectiveness to consider is the rate of attrition of graduates of the program. After three years, how many graduates have left the teaching profession? After five years, how many graduates have left the teaching profession? The substantial effort and expense expended on the part of future teachers dictates that their success in the classroom be a measure of accountability for teacher education programs.

SUMMARY

As outlined in this chapter, assessment data for interns includes feedback from general education course instructors as well as feedback and performance assessments from methods course instructors. Teacher work samples offer promise as a performance assessment for documenting the impact of the intern on the learning of students. Formative and summative assessment by trained university supervisors and mentor teachers is the best assurance of the competence of the intern.

Almost all teacher education programs collect a great deal of data about their candidates. The challenge is to utilize the data systematically to improve the quality of the program. This is especially important in the area of student teaching and other field experiences. In student teaching, not only is the learning of the intern involved, but also the learning of P–12 students can be impacted positively or negatively by the involvement of interns in the classroom.

APPLYING WHAT YOU HAVE LEARNED

Video 3.1

In this video, https://youtu.be/vYL0HDkWKIo, mentor teachers in a training session are practicing the use of a university's intern lesson assessment form using a lesson from the popular television show, *The Big Bang Theory*, https://www.youtube.com/watch?v=AEIn3T6nDAo. As you observe the video, look for how the mentors are engaged in the assessment task and how they are interacting with one another.

Video 3.2

In this video, https://youtu.be/zPZDwHtbneM, an intern and her mentor teacher participate in a summative conference at the end of the intern's PDS experience. As you view the video, look for the following elements of the intern's reflection: challenges of working in two different classrooms (middle school and a third/fourth grade combination class), strategies that the intern used that worked well for her, and what the intern feels are the most important things she learned in her PDS experiences.

NOTES

1. http://www.edutopia.org/schools-of-education-emporia
2. http://www.cmu.edu/teaching/assessment/assessprogram/
3. https://scale.stanford.edu/system/files/WeiPecheone.pdf
4. https://www.beloit.edu/education/assets/STAssesRubricsRvsdS15.pdf
5. Rubenstein, G. (2007). *Building a Better Teacher: Confronting the Crisis in Teacher Training*. Retrieved from www.edutopia.org/node/4992/print
6. https://www.uco.edu/ceps/files/tes/ST/Evaluation/Student%20Teacher%20Assessment%20of%20Mentor%20Teacher.pdf
7. https://www.uco.edu/ceps/files/tes/ST/Evaluation/Student%20Teacher%20Assessment%20of%20Supervisor.pdf
8. www.aabri.com/manuscripts/10665.pdf
9. National Council for Accreditation of Teacher Education. (2002). *Professional Standards for the Accreditation of Schools, Colleges, and Departments of Education*. Washington, DC: National Council for Accreditation of Teacher Education.
10. http://education.illinoisstate.edu/teacher_education/gateway1/dccassessment.shtml
11. Voneschenbach, J. F. and Gile, W. B. (2007). "Dispositions for Teacher Education Candidates." *School-University Partnerships* 1(1), 72–79.
12. http://www.emporia.edu/dotAsset/7231e6b1-e9c4-426e-a4c7-201831fb334c.pdf
13. http://www.ced.csulb.edu/documents/mscp-self-assessment-dispositions-teaching
14. http://tes.eku.edu/sites/tes.eku.edu/files/files/TES%20Student%20Teaching%20Documents/DRAKE_STUDENT_TEACHER_SELF_EVALUATION.pdf
15. Renaissance Partnership Project. (2008 January, 14). *Renaissance Teacher Work Samples*. Retrieved from www.uni.edu/itq/RTWS/index/htm
16. http://www.wku.edu/rtwsc/
17. http://www.bhsu.edu/Portals/0/coeducation/teacherworksample/TWS_Handbook_July_2014.pdf
18. Levine, A. (2006). *Educating School Teachers*. Washington, DC: The Education Schools Project.
19. https://www.nmu.edu/education/guide-student-teaching-supervision
20. http://www.wpunj.edu/coe/departments/professional-development-schoolcommunity-partnership/governance.dot

Chapter Four

Planning and Sequencing

Planning and organizing the intern's time in the classroom is a crucial element in providing opportunities for success. When a mentor demonstrates time management and instructional planning skills, these skills are much easier for the intern to learn and the clinical experience runs more smoothly. Following a specific plan for sequencing the clinical experience helps ensure that an intern's time in the assignment will be beneficial for the intern, for the mentor, and for the students in the classroom.

TIME MANAGEMENT

One of the most challenging elements in teaching is time management.[1] Teachers are expected[2] to manage an instructional program with ever-increasing content and expectations, relate positively with students, communicate effectively with parents, and serve as collegial members of school improvement teams. Teachers also need to balance[3] out-of-school responsibilities such as family and friends and finding time for health and wellness activities.

For these reasons, the decision to become a mentor[4] and adding additional responsibilities to an already challenging load needs to be made with care. Potential mentor teachers who already feel they are "stretched to the limit" must think carefully about accepting the responsibility of working with an intern. Although interns are often able to provide valuable assistance in the classroom, developing a positive, professional relationship with the intern, planning and organizing his or her experiences in the classroom, and supervising can require a significant commitment of time and energy.

Although the amount of time available to mentors for performing their many roles and responsibilities is limited, the ways in which the time is utilized are not. Some strategies for effective time management[5] include organizing, prioritizing, reducing paperwork, and taking time for relaxation and reflection. Considerable teaching time can be lost when organization is lacking. For example, poor digital filing systems can make it difficult to retrieve needed materials quickly. Keeping track of current and future commitments with a frequently updated digital calendar helps the teacher anticipate and schedule appropriately. Modeling this for an intern can save his or her valuable time in future professional activities. Teachers who do not utilize effective strategies for organizing information and tasks may feel even more frustrated when adding the demands of working with an intern

Prioritizing is another time-management skill required of teachers. It is important that students in the classroom are the mentor's first priority. Basic responsibilities are not always discretionary, but accepting other tasks such as committee assignments, extracurricular duties, and community projects should be considered carefully. In addition, teachers must also find time for family, friends, and personal commitments. Helping an intern recognize the importance of weighing outside commitments carefully during teaching should be part of the professional experience.

A problem for many teachers is effectively dealing with significant amounts of paperwork[6] which are required by a multitude of agencies, government regulations, district and building expectations, and student record keeping. It is important for the mentor to model effective strategies for the intern for reducing the number of papers that the teacher deals with, such as the amount of paperwork submitted by students. It is certainly important to check for student understanding frequently, but this does not always require the completion of a paper-and-pencil task that must be graded.

Checking for understanding[7] while students are working in class and assessing students in different ways can reduce the number of papers and still provide needed feedback to students about their performance. Most effective teachers develop grading systems that allow flexibility for reviewing student work. Modeling this for an intern is essential. Time management strategies must be discussed throughout an intern's experience.

Although it may seem contradictory to suggest time for reflection and relaxation as strategies for time management, teachers who do not engage in these important activities will usually be less productive. All teachers need time to reflect about their teaching.[8] Such reflection helps teachers prioritize and maintain a positive, constructive attitude toward their profession.[9] Part of every successful clinical experience requires professional and personal reflection by the intern. Mentor teachers who demonstrate reflection will encourage that behavior by the intern.

Both interns and mentors work under considerable pressure in their teaching roles. Managing stress, including taking time for relaxation and appropriate wellness activities,[10] helps the teacher maintain the focus and balance essential for successful interactions with students and other colleagues. As in many other areas, mentor teachers serve as a positive or negative example for interns in the area of time management, reflection, and stress management.

INSTRUCTIONAL PLANNING

Effective instructional planning is a hallmark of effective teaching. Since the historical trend in education has been to add requirements to curriculum without subtracting other content, teachers are faced with incredible responsibilities today. Educational goals, standards, and levels of accountability have multiplied almost exponentially at national, state, and local levels. At the same time, the inclusion of students with wide-ranging academic and social needs makes the teaching of an expanded curriculum even more challenging.[11] Rapid changes in technology provide additional challenges for teachers.

Long-range planning by teachers helps to ensure that required curriculum outcomes can be addressed in the classroom. The mentor teacher's philosophy, classroom rules, procedures and routines, and arrangement of the classroom must be carefully considered by good teachers and should become the foundation for curriculum planning and implementation.[12] Because the intern will not know how these important elements of planning were established, the mentor must outline and describe reasons for these basic planning decisions.

In order to work with an intern effectively, the mentor must carefully analyze the required curriculum standards for the grade level and subject areas the intern will be teaching. Developing a long-range instructional plan for meeting these objectives throughout the academic year is necessary. An effective long-range plan includes a timeline for working on outcomes in each subject area. Curriculum materials, including textbooks and other resources used in achieving positive outcomes, should also be identified. Dates for mandated district and state testing and times for reviewing need to be noted as part of the long-term planning process.[13] Sharing these strategies with interns will assist them in present and future instructional planning and help sequence activities in the intern's clinical experience.

Once planning decisions have been made, the mentor teacher and intern can identify specific content and outcomes each will be responsible for. Once the intern becomes familiar with required content, formulating appropriate plans for instruction and identifying additional resources for teaching can occur. Often, beginning educators struggle with deciding what important topics or concepts to teach. The mentor can assist in guiding the intern's selection of content in the early stages of the experience.

Developing effective lesson plans[14] is an essential skill for interns. At the beginning of the clinical experience, the intern will usually write more detailed lesson plans which are reviewed by the mentor teacher before teaching takes place. As the intern's skill in planning, implementing, and assessing increases, the written lesson plan may become more concise.

SEQUENCING THE CLINICAL EXPERIENCE

Beginning the Experience

At the beginning of the clinical experience, the mentor teacher has three important tasks: getting acquainted with the intern; sharing expectations, philosophy, and concerns; and sharing necessary information about the school, classroom, and students. Most interns come into a new experience with some anxiety. By sharing expectations and information with the intern, the acclimation and transition into teaching will be more successful.

Foyle, Morehead, and Lyman have identified five key behaviors of mentors that can assist future teachers in the beginning of their experience. These behaviors are friendliness, openness, warm regard, listening, and empathy.[15] These behaviors are essential in creating the positive relationships with interns which were discussed in Chapter 2.

By encouraging the intern to share appropriate personal and professional information, the mentor demonstrates friendliness and warm regard. Suggestions for personal and professional discussion items can be found in Table 4.1. Becoming aware of the intern's background, interests, and skills helps the mentor determine how to work with the intern effectively.

Table 4.1. Beginning Conferences with Interns

Things to Ask the Intern

1. Ask about the intern's professional background.
2. Ask the intern why he or she chose teaching for a profession.
3. Ask about previous experiences with children in a professional setting.
4. Ask what his or her biggest fear or concern is regarding teaching.
5. Ask what his or her strengths are.
6. Ask about high school, college activities and favorite subjects.
7. Ask about hobbies and interests.
8. Ask what subject or subjects he or she would like to teach first.
9. Ask if the intern has any questions or concerns and encourage the intern to ask questions as they arise.

Several issues need to be discussed with the intern early in the experience. Taking time to clarify expectations, rules, and procedures helps prevent confusion and frustration. The List of Behaviors Clarifying the Mentor Teacher's Expectations from Chapter 2 will be useful here. Materials such as the school handbook can provide helpful supplemental information. It is especially important that the intern clearly understands discipline, confidentiality, and reporting policies before working with students.

Early conferences with the intern will primarily be directed by the mentor. Although the mentor teacher should encourage the intern to share information and ask questions, it is important that the mentor make expectations and necessary information clear to the intern (see Table 4.2). Clarifying expectations about minor issues early in the experience such as punctuality and attendance allows both parties the opportunity to discuss more significant issues later. The university supervisor can assist both the mentor and the intern with identifying the issues which need to be discussed at the beginning of the clinical experience.

During the first meeting with the intern and mentor, the university supervisor should verify that the intern has met all the requirements for the placement and that the mentor has all of the necessary information from the university. By making an introductory visit early in the assignment, the supervisor ensures that the placement is appropriate and that the mentor and intern have information needed regarding the assignment. It is important that both the intern and the mentor receive information on how to contact the supervisor. A date for the next visit should be identified and a tentative schedule for all visits by the supervisor must be discussed. The university supervisor also

Table 4.2. Topics to Cover in Initial Conferences

1. Share personal and professional background information.
2. Share philosophy and expectations. Be sure to mention pet peeves.
3. Clarify expectations for dress, arrival time, confidentiality, reporting of child abuse, and school and classroom rules and procedures.
4. Take the intern on a tour of the school and introduce him or her to colleagues, the principal, secretary, appropriate support personnel, and custodians during the first week he or she is in the building.
5. Discuss classroom management procedures and expectations for the intern with respect to discipline.
6. Discuss activities for the first two weeks of school.
7. Develop a schedule for teaching and for conferencing with the intern.
8. Give a brief overview of what is known about students the intern will be working with. Do not share negative information at this time.
9. Discuss lesson planning requirements and dates on which plans are due.

needs to share expectations for the intern, especially in the areas of lesson planning, attendance, substitutes in the classroom, and professional behavior.

A useful resource for mentors and interns is the university's policy and procedures manual[16] for clinical experiences. This resource needs to be carefully organized to provide easy access to information for mentors and interns about expectations, planning and sequencing, and assessment instruments which are part of the intern's clinical experience. Although intern orientation and mentor teacher training need to be provided before the intern's experiences begin, providing a resource for the inevitable questions that occur "on the job" is important. Of course, the intern and mentor should always be aware that the university supervisor is available for assistance as needed.

During the first two weeks in the classroom, mentors should provide opportunities for guided observation of the students. Guided observation helps the intern become familiar with the students and classroom while settling in. A guide for classroom observation, such as the one found in Table 4.3, can provide specific things for the intern to look for.

Table 4.3. Classroom Observation Guide

During the first two weeks of school, most interns benefit from guided observation tasks, which help them become oriented to the students, teacher, and classroom. The intern should observe and interact with students as directed by the mentor teacher and answer as many of the questions as possible. When the intern has completed the observation process, the intern and mentor teacher should conference to determine the accuracy of the future teacher's observations and conclusions.

1. How does the mentor teacher make students feel welcome on the first day of class? How does the mentor teacher involve students during the first week of class so that students feel as though they are a part of the class?
2. How does the mentor teacher reduce student anxiety and fear during the first days of class?
3. How does the teacher get to know students before they arrive in class and during the first days of class?
4. What are the classroom and school rules for students? What is the role of the intern in classroom discipline and management?
5. How does the mentor teacher positively reinforce desired student behaviors in the classroom?
6. How does the mentor teacher check to make sure that students understand what has been taught?
7. How are groups established? Why does the mentor teacher group students?
8. Which students appear to be leaders in the classroom? How do you know?
9. Which students have good verbal skills? How do you know?
10. Which students seem to learn quickly and easily? How do you know?
11. Which students appear to be socially skilled in the classroom? How do you know?
12. Which students appear to be shy and reticent? How do you know?

Table 4.3 *(continued)*

13. Which students appear to have difficulty getting along with others? How do you know?
14. Which students need extra help to understand and participate appropriately? All the time or only in certain subjects? What do these students do when they are frustrated? How do you know?
15. Which students appear to need more attention (positive or negative) from the mentor teacher and the intern than others? How do these students get the attention they want? How do they react if they do not get the attention they want? How do you know?
16. What other interesting or unexpected things have been observed?

Table 4.4. Structured Interview Questions for Interns to Use with Students

1. Tell me about your family. Brothers and sisters? Pets?
2. Have you always lived here? What other places have you lived?
3. What are you good at?
4. What is your favorite subject in school?
5. What gives you the most trouble in school?
6. What are you looking forward to this year?
7. What are you nervous about this year?
8. What do you like to do outside of school?
9. What is the best book you ever read?
10. What do you think makes somebody a good teacher?

Taking time to review the intern's observations during a weekly conference can help mentors evaluate important factors such as an intern's perceptions of the classroom and students, accuracy of the intern's observations, and "with-it-ness."[17] Observations made by the intern that differ from those of the mentor can facilitate discussion and allow for clarification.

Occasionally, the discussion of the observation guide will alert the mentor that an intern has made errors in observing or interacting with students during the initial days of the assignment. Discussing the observations early in an experience may assist the mentor in pointing out the potential challenges for the intern and possibly alleviate potential problems. If concerns arise, it is appropriate to visit with the university supervisor to clarify questions and concerns. If an intern is not aware of students' interactions, behaviors, and attentiveness, serious classroom management issues could emerge later.

Another appropriate task for the intern during the first two weeks of the assignment is to briefly interview students in the class. At the secondary level, it might be just a few students in each class. A list of possible interview questions can be found in the Table 4.4. These brief interviews can help the interns gain valuable information about the personalities, learning styles, and interests of students. Mentors should encourage interns to share any interesting or unexpected things discovered during the interviews. This information can be valuable to the mentor as well. Interviews will also enhance the interpersonal relations of an intern with students in the class.

Few interns will be satisfied by only observing and interviewing during the first two weeks of their assignments. Mentor teachers should also provide opportunities for interns to assume responsibility for routine classroom tasks, such as taking attendance, completing calendar activities, reading to students, or working with small groups. A simple project at the elementary level, such as creating a bulletin board of self-portraits created by students in the class, can be satisfying. Getting started on lesson planning is also appropriate during the first few weeks of the assignment.

The approach mentors use when introducing the intern to the class can be an important factor in determining success. By presenting the intern to the students as a teacher rather than a *student* teacher, the mentor signals it is expected that the class treat the intern with the same respect accorded all teachers and other adults in the classroom and school.

The mentor should also let parents and guardians know there is another teacher working in the classroom. Parents and guardians may be curious or concerned if their child tells them about an intern they are unfamiliar with. This is especially true in elementary classrooms.

It is helpful during the first two weeks of the assignment to have a brief, daily conference. This brief conference provides an opportunity for the intern to ask questions or express concerns or frustrations. It is important to encourage the intern to ask questions about routines in the classroom, student behavior and attitudes, and the mentor's instructional and behavior decisions. If the mentor is reluctant to ask questions and does not seem to be able to analyze the classroom, students, and teaching, this may be a concern to share with the university supervisor.

Daily conferences also allow the mentor an opportunity to clarify expectations and deal directly with any issues that might be of concern, such as an intern not being punctual or not completing assigned tasks in a timely manner. Conferences early in the semester will give the mentor teacher an opportunity to address these concerns before they become problematic.

GETTING THE INTERN MORE INVOLVED IN THE CLASSROOM

By the third week, most interns are ready to take over at least one subject area. As part of the plan for sequencing the assignment, the mentor will help the intern determine the appropriate subject area to work with and clarify planning expectations. In a middle school or secondary assignment, the intern may work with a particular class period. Sometimes interns are given too much responsibility too early. The old model of *sink or swim* is not acceptable. It is important that the intern is not given responsibilities for which he or she is not ready.

Some interns will need a little more time to adjust to the classroom before assuming responsibilities for the whole class. These interns may benefit from working with a small group of students first, such as a reading group in an elementary classroom. Middle and high school interns may work with cooperative groups to help students with problems or answer questions. These types of introductory activities are appropriate for all interns, but some will take longer to become prepared for whole class teaching. Professional judgment of the mentor is essential in this first phase and can have a significant impact on future success.

Each weekly conference with the intern should include collaborative planning for additional responsibilities to be assumed by the intern during the coming week. During this time, it is usually helpful for the mentor to carefully review the written plans for teaching with the intern and outline expectations for planning and implementing.

As the intern begins to have direct responsibility for planning and teaching, it is important for the mentor to be in the classroom. This provides an opportunity to note examples of positive communication with students, appropriate instructional practices, and good management strategies as they are observed. These desired behaviors can be reinforced in a brief, daily conference. This feedback in the early stages will be beneficial for both participants. First, trust will be enhanced by this communication. Second, clarification of expectations by the mentor related to instruction will enhance the intern's performance. Finally, it should encourage the use of effective classroom management strategies for the intern.

It is also important for the mentor to record any concerns or changes the intern should make while teaching. Specific suggestions for change should be discussed before the intern works with the students again. If a mentor observes that the intern successfully incorporates suggestions into future instruction, it is especially important to reinforce the practice.

Based on the intern's progress, additional subject areas or academic periods should be added to his or her responsibilities in preparation for full-time teaching. The length of full-time teaching is often negotiable, but usually works best for three or four weeks. Some mentors are reluctant to give up their classroom for extended periods of time but full-time teaching is essential during the clinical experience. Early in the experience, the intern may use the mentor teacher's materials and lessons.

If, at any time, the mentor teacher is concerned that the intern is not progressing as expected, it is essential to confer with the university supervisor. By notifying the supervisor, his input and expertise can be utilized if it becomes necessary to make changes to the experience. It is always better to discuss any concerns as early as possible.

From the third week of the assignment until the midpoint, the intern should be accepting additional responsibilities for planning and teaching. The mentor can usually be giving less specific feedback about lesson plans as the intern evidences the ability to plan more appropriately. As the intern does more teaching, he or she should reflect on their planning and teaching and be able to reflect on ideas for improvement with the mentor.

As an intern assumes more responsibility for planning and instruction, it is common for him or her to feel overwhelmed and anxious about the responsibilities of teaching. These feelings may come, in part, from the intern's ongoing comparison of himself or herself to the mentor teacher or other master teachers.[18] Positive and specific reinforcement from the mentor will help relieve anxiety. An excellent strategy is to use affirmation statements, discussed in chapter 2, to express the mentor's confidence in the intern. If an intern appears to be dealing with stress ineffectively, the mentor should discuss his or her perception with the intern and help them identify strategies for coping more effectively. Most universities have counseling programs available which may be able to provide assistance.

As the intern assumes increasing responsibility in the classroom, lessons should be observed to assess how the intern is handling classroom management. An intern's awareness of student misbehavior, ability to anticipate problems before they occur, and use of positive, effective strategies to deal with minor behavior problems should be observed. Feedback on the intern's classroom management and strategies for improving classroom management will be a regular part of each conference with the intern.

During the early stages of an assignment, it is important to help the intern identify and use appropriate strategies related to classroom management. It is important not to leave the intern alone in the classroom for more than brief periods of time until the mentor is convinced that he or she can handle discipline effectively. The intern should not be left alone for hall or playground duty until the mentor has observed that they are ready for this responsibility.

As they teach lessons, interns should demonstrate increasing skill in planning, teaching, and assessing. Specific feedback about teaching decisions needs to be provided for the intern during lesson evaluations and during the weekly conference. Some mentors prefer to write a brief note to the intern after observing a lesson to identify what has gone well and what should be changed. This strategy can provide prompt feedback to the future teacher and furnish a record of the strengths and weaknesses that can be shared with a university supervisor during her visit to the classroom. All feedback needs to be specific and focus on one or two key themes. Discussing more than one or two issues can seem overwhelming to the intern.

THE MIDPOINT ASSESSMENT

The midpoint of the intern's experience should be marked by a summative evaluation of strengths and weaknesses. Both the university supervisor and the mentor teacher may be required to submit an assessment of the intern's progress at the midpoint. At the midpoint, the university may also request that the mentor assign a letter grade to the intern's progress to date. At this time, in fairness to all parties, it is expected that any serious concerns be shared with the intern. Due process and general, professional expectations warrant such disclosure during the midpoint assessment.

The summative evaluation at the midpoint of the assignment should reflect the information that has been provided to the intern during lesson evaluations and weekly conferences. There should be no surprises for the intern during this assessment since the purpose of a summative assessment is to provide a summary of the formative assessments which have taken place to date. If the summative assessment is not as positive as desired, the mentor teacher may wish to have the university supervisor sit in on the conference where the assessment is discussed with the intern. The university supervisor can assist in formulating a specific plan for improvement.

Not overrating the progress of the intern at this point in the experience is important. Strengths will, of course, be discussed, with specific examples so the intern can continue to grow professionally. It is also important, however, to help the intern set goals for improvement during the remainder of the experience. Even when the intern is making exemplary progress, a plan to continue professional growth and development is essential.

Any discussion of weaknesses may make the intern uncomfortable and can influence the intern's future attitude toward supervisors. The mentor needs to help the intern to understand that teachers are expected to demonstrate growth throughout their careers. Using feedback to promote professional growth is an expectation for all teachers. In order to help ensure trust, openness, and continued respect with the intern, mentors and university supervisors need to identify strengths, even with struggling interns, and reaffirm their belief in the potential success of the intern.

The midpoint assessment provides an important opportunity for the mentor to help the intern have a clear understanding of the mentor's assessment of their progress to date and the expectations for improvement during the final portion of the assignment. By being clear about concerns or problems at this time, the intern has an opportunity to improve so that the remainder of the assignment can be productive and the summative assessment at the end can be as positive as possible.

Sometime during this midpoint, a substantive transition should begin to emerge in an intern's professional growth. As conferences continue, an intern who is maturing professionally should be moving from a survival mode to a role as teacher. This can best be determined by listening to the intern's comments about teaching and observing his interactions with students. The focus should now be on "learning and needs of children" and not on the interns themselves.[19] If this focus on students and their learning is not evident, then this is a serious indication that an intern's professional growth is not occurring adequately. The university supervisor and mentor should discuss their concerns and continue to monitor the intern's progress in making this important transition.

THE FINAL WEEKS OF THE CLINICAL EXPERIENCE

During the second half of the experience, most interns will continue to assume more responsibility for planning and teaching in the classroom. During the final weeks of the experience, the mentor's weekly conferences will usually change. In the early weeks of an assignment, mentors are usually more directive, providing specific reinforcement and suggestions for modification of teaching as appropriate. Later in the experience, mentors will encourage interns to take a more active part in weekly conferences, accepting more responsibility for assessing their own performance and identifying strategies for improvement.[20]

Clarification and brainstorming strategies help the mentor to actively involve the intern in analyzing his or her performance and to facilitate more interaction with the mentor. The goal of conferences with competent and excellent interns during the final weeks is to cause more reflection about their teaching.[21] When reflecting on their teaching, interns need to be able to identify what is going well, as well as identify problems and strategies for dealing with those problems. This process of reflection is an integral part of professional growth necessary for success of the intern.

Weekly formative conferences with the intern should focus on refining instructional strategies, utilizing varied methods of assessment, differentiating instruction to meet the needs of diverse students, and anticipating problems that may occur. Written lesson plans may be less detailed if the intern has evidenced the ability to plan appropriately, yet it is important to continue to discuss short- and long-term goals. By this time, pacing of lessons and an ability to determine how quickly students complete assignments should be an acquired skill. If the intern is still having difficulty with these issues, comprehensive daily planning may still be required.

An important strategy to assist in evaluation performance is the use of video recordings of lessons. Some interns balk at the idea of videotaping because they feel uncomfortable watching themselves. However, there are few better techniques for any educator to get realistic feedback on strengths and weaknesses related to the teaching process. Mentors may give an intern the choice of viewing the videotape privately or with the mentor present.

After viewing the video recording of the lesson, the interns should write a reflection about what they learned from viewing their teaching performance. Video recordings can provide feedback about nonverbal cues, movement in the classroom, possible student behaviors missed, inconsistency in feedback, checking for understanding, and pacing of the lesson. It is helpful for the mentor to read the intern's reflection to make sure the intern has identified strengths as well as areas for improvement after viewing their recording.

As discussed earlier, the focus of the intern should change as the experience progresses. At the beginning, most interns tend to focus on themselves and what they are doing. Sharing personal feelings and reactions at this time is most important when visiting with the mentor. With most competent and excellent interns, this self-centered focus will change during the clinical experience. The focus changes from being preoccupied with how they are doing to what is happening and how the students are reacting to instructions. This may be one of the best informal assessments of the intern's readiness for his or her own classroom. To observe this change in focus is an excellent indication that appropriate professional growth is transpiring.

CONCLUDING THE EXPERIENCE

As the intern's assignment concludes, there are several experiences that can be helpful. These include participation in parent conferences, the opportunity for feedback from an administrator or other mentor teacher, and observing in other classrooms. Participating in parent–teacher conferences[22] is an important experience for interns. Numerous studies conducted by Morehead indicate that first-year teachers feel inadequate in their preparation relating to issues concerning parents and parent–teacher conferences. The opportunity to participate in parent–teacher conferences helps interns to view how their mentor communicates with parents and provides invaluable information about the students with whom the intern is working.

Depending on the competence and confidence of the intern, the mentor may allow the intern to take the lead in some of the conferences. Before conferences occur, goals and appropriate methods used to share information should be discussed, and a plan for the meeting with parents should be reviewed. It is especially important for the intern to learn ways to deal with difficult parents in a positive, professional manner. Reminding an intern that each parent conference should start with a positive comment and focus on only one or two key issues at a time provides a helpful strategy for interns to use in future conferences with parents. Although the issue of confidentiality will have been discussed early in the intern's experience, it is always a good idea to remind the intern that any information from parent–teacher conferences is absolutely confidential.

Feedback from a professional other than the mentor teacher and university supervisor can be helpful to the intern. It is a good idea for the intern to invite the principal, assistant principal, or another mentor teacher to observe a lesson and provide feedback. This gives the intern another point of view about teaching strengths and weaknesses and may help to build confidence for observations by administrators in the intern's own classroom later on. Some principals are also willing to conduct mock interviews with interns and give them feedback about conferencing skills that will be helpful in seeking a teaching position.

Assuming that the intern has made appropriate progress during the clinical experience, it is often helpful for the intern to visit a few other classrooms during the last week his or her assignment. Such visits provide opportunities to see different styles of teaching and management and to see different ages of students. Some interns may already have a teaching position by the end of their clinical assignment and may wish to observe in the school in which they will be working.

As the experience concludes, planning for a smooth transition of the mentor's full-time return to teaching should occur. It is usually helpful for the intern to *give back* responsibility for teaching subjects or academic periods as they were assigned beginning a few weeks before the end of the assignment. By the final week of an experience, the intern's teaching responsibilities will be usually be completed.

At the conclusion of the experience, the mentor has several important tasks. First, having a summative evaluation conference reviewing the intern's progress, completing the final assessment form, and assigning a grade will be necessary. The final university evaluation should focus on successes and is intended to help the intern grow professionally and should indicate areas for improvement.

Additionally, a mentor will be asked by the intern to complete a reference letter for a placement file, which will be sent to a university placement office or may be given to the intern electronically to be included with applications for teaching positions. While it is the mentor's responsibility to complete the required university evaluation of an intern, there may be a time when a mentor chooses not to provide a letter of reference for the intern.

Mentors sometimes find it challenging to write a reference letter for an intern. The following are some suggestions for writing an effective reference letter:

Four Paragraph Format

Paragraph 1: Sentence summarizing the intern's assignment. Sentences describing characteristics and traits, such as enthusiasm, creativity, willingness to work hard, rapport with students, staff, and parents

Paragraph 2: Sentences describing planning and organizational skills, ability to evaluate effectively, ability to use a variety of methods and strategies, develop and implement appropriate instructional objectives

Paragraph 3: Sentences describing ability to motivate and manage students, ability to keep students interested and involved, provide for individual student differences

Paragraph 4: Overall summary of the clinical experience, prediction for success of intern in full-time teaching

The following examples can be helpful in qualifying statements.

Qualifying Words

usually, often, sometimes, occasionally, may, with (conditions), probably, shows the potential to

Qualifying Statements

Strong Performance: Miss Smith demonstrated excellent rapport with students.

Qualified Statement: Miss Smith usually demonstrated excellent rapport with students.

Strong Performance: Miss Smith managed incidents of classroom misbehavior appropriately and fairly.

Qualified Statement: Miss Smith often managed incidents of classroom misbehavior appropriately and fairly.

Strong Performance: Miss Smith will do well in future teaching.

Qualified Statement: Miss Smith may do well in future teaching. Miss Smith may do well in future teaching if provided with strong guidance and supervision.

The following descriptive words can be used when developing reference letters or writing final evaluations for that university.

Excellent Performance: *extraordinary, excellent, distinguished, superb, exceptional, special, superior, noteworthy, notable, extensive, outstanding*

Good Performance: *good, capable, competent, effective, appropriate, proper, favorable, above average, positive, productive*

Fair Performance: *adequate, sufficient, suitable, fair, satisfactory, acceptable, average, passable, ordinary*

Poor Performance: *below standard, unprepared, inadequate, weak, unqualified, unacceptable, unfit, inappropriate*

If the intern has had a positive experience, it is important that he have the mentor teacher's school and home contact information to add to his professional resume. This will allow prospective employers a contact point if they should have questions about this potential employee. Many employers will contact a mentor teacher when making an employment decision.

The ending conference in most situations is a celebration of a job well done. Unlike the first conferences, which were controlled primarily by the mentor, the final conference should be a professional dialogue about teaching. The intern should be encouraged to reflect on what went well during the experience and how those strengths may be used in future teaching. Encouraging the intern to reflect on highlights of the semester and things he or she finds most memorable helps promote the celebration.

In a final conference, open-ended questions help to ensure that the intern is an active participant in the conference. As the experience concludes, interns should be encouraged to analyze the kinds of instructional methods and strategies they successfully used, provide examples of professionalism exhibited, and identify areas to improve. The intern should also be encouraged to focus on knowledge of teaching techniques, subject matter, celebration of success, and goal setting for the future.[23]

At the end of a successful experience, mentors may want to make sure they have contact information so they can keep in touch with the intern. Because many interns move at the end of their experience, a permanent address such as the parents' should be shared with the mentor. It is a good idea to remind the mentor that in case of a name change due to marriage, the mentor needs to be notified if they are serving as a professional reference for the intern.

SUMMARY

A successful clinical experience depends on planning which is facilitated by the mentor and university supervisor. Mentors who are good managers of time and demonstrate effective planning skills are best equipped to help interns. At the beginning of the clinical experience, the mentor needs to be direct, making sure expectations and needed information are understood and provided. A sequence for having the intern assume teaching and responsibilities needs to be developed and shared with both the intern and university supervisor. The progress of the intern, as discussed in frequent formative conferences, may result in modifying this plan.

Ideally, an intern will become increasingly reflective and able to evaluate their own performance throughout the experience. Feedback is crucial to the intern's optimal professional growth at all stages of the experience. Continuing to share observations about the intern's performance, interactions, and growth throughout the experience will help make the assignment and future teaching successful.

APPLYING WHAT YOU HAVE LEARNED

Video 4.1

In this video, https://youtu.be/ZUca4yxW438, you will observe a beginning conference between and intern and her mentor teacher. As you watch the conference, identify the information which the mentor encourages the intern to share about herself. Then, identify the information that the mentor shares with the intern about his classroom and approach to teaching.

Video 4.2

In this video, https://youtu.be/VvoOwUuFLVs, you will observe a conference at the end of an intern's clinical experience. How does the intern demonstrate that she is able to analyze her teaching performance? What successful things does she identify which occurred during the experience?

NOTES

1. Lyman, L. (2000, February). "A Professor Returns to the Classroom in a Professional Development School." ERIC Resources in Education. Paper presented at the national conference of the Kansas University Professional Development Schools Alliance, Kansas City, Missouri.
2. http://www.time-management-success.com/frustrated-and-overloaded-high-school-teacher-with-too-many-hats.html
3. http://www.mindfulteachers.org/2014/02/striving-for-worklife-balance-5-great.html
4. http://blogs.edweek.org/edweek/finding_common_ground/2014/08/are_you_prepared_to_be_a_cooperating_teacher.html
5. http://www.scholastic.com/teachers/article/time-management-strategies
6. https://www.teachervision.com/classroom-management/new-teacher/48352.html
7. http://www.edutopia.org/blog/dipsticks-to-check-for-understanding-todd-finley

8. http://www.ascd.org/publications/educational-leadership/feb09/vol66/num05/Fostering-Reflection.aspx

9. Ganser, T. (1997, March). "The Contribution of Service as a Cooperating Teacher and Mentor Teacher to the Professional Development of Teachers." Proceedings from the American Educational Research Association, Chicago, 1–62.

10. http://www.naesp.org/principal-janfeb-2013-teacher-staff-development/teacher-wellness-conversation-adam-s-enz

11. Azwell, T. S., Foyle, H. C., Lyman, L., and Smith, N. L. (1999). *Constructing curriculum in context*. Dubuque, Iowa: Kendall/Hunt.

12. Azwell, T. S., Foyle, H. C., Lyman, L., and Smith, N. L. (1999). *Constructing curriculum in context*. Dubuque, Iowa: Kendall/Hunt.

13. Azwell, T. S., Foyle, H. C., Lyman, L., and Smith, N. L. (1999). *Constructing curriculum in context*. Dubuque, Iowa: Kendall/Hunt.

14. http://teachingasleadership.org/sites/default/files/Related-Readings/IPD_Ch4_2011.pdf

15. Foyle, H. C., Morehead, M. A., and Lyman, L. (1992). "Conferencing with student teachers: The beginning conference." New York: Insight Media, videotape.

16. https://www.emporia.edu/dotAsset/7231e6b1-e9c4-426e-a4c7-201831fb334c.pdf

17. Charles, C. M. (1989). *Building classroom discipline from models to practice*. New York: Longman, 27–39.

18. Caruso, J. J. (2000, January). "Cooperating teacher and student teacher phases of development." *Young Children* 55(1), 75–81.

19. Caruso, J. J. (2000, January). "Cooperating teacher and student teacher phases of development." *Young Children* 55(1), 75–81.

20. Cooper, J. M. (1995). "Supervision in teacher education." *International Encyclopedia of Teaching and Teacher Education*, 593–598.

21. Zeichner, K. and Liston, D. P. (1987). "Teaching student teachers to reflect." *Harvard Educational Review* 57, 23–48.

22. http://www.edutopia.org/blog/parent-teacher-conference-resources-matt-davis

23. Foyle, H. C., Morehead, M. A., and Lyman, L. (1992). "Conferencing with student teachers: The beginning conference." New York: Insight Media, videotape.

Chapter Five

Supervising the Intern

Appropriate supervision of the future teacher is essential for positive, professional growth. Quality supervision depends on the ability of mentor teachers and university supervisors to build a positive, professional relationship with the intern and to plan and organize the intern's professional activities efficiently. Effective supervisors have the ability to collect necessary data about the intern's performance and reflect on it during formative and summative conferences.[1] Supervisors need to be skillful in reinforcing appropriate behaviors and attitudes while helping the intern clarify decision-making processes. Brainstorming solutions to instructional and behavior problems and remediating areas of weakness or concern are also essential for successful supervision.

TWO MODELS OF SUPERVISION

The model of supervision utilized by mentors and university supervisors impacts the way they interact with interns. Although many models of supervision exist, most can be summarized as models of either congruency or discrepancy. Both models can theoretically improve the performance and professional growth of an intern, but the congruency model tends to result in more positive attitudes toward the supervision process.[2]

Mentors and supervisors who use congruency as a model for supervision want to identify areas of strength[3] in performance. The supervisor looks for actions that are effective examples of planning, teaching, and assessing. When conferring with the intern, the supervisor emphasizes the positive aspects of performance and identifies strengths whenever possible.

Supervisors who use a discrepancy model concentrate on areas of weakness in performance. The supervisor looks for actions that are not producing learning or are interfering with student learning. When conferencing, the supervisor emphasizes the aspects of the intern's performance that are inhibiting student achievement. The focus of the supervisory conference is on weaknesses and how they can be modified. While this approach is sometimes necessary to change ineffective intern behaviors, using a congruency model is most productive for most interns.

When mentors and supervisors use a congruency model of supervision, conferences are more positive because the intern gains confidence from knowing what is being done well. When the intern understands which of his or her practices are congruent with effective teaching, he or she is more likely to use such methods more often in future teaching, both in the present assignment and eventually in his or her own classroom. Perhaps the most important benefit of supervising in a caring, positive manner is that the interns are more likely to respond similarly to their own students.[4]

The congruency model is most helpful throughout the intern's experience and is primarily formative in approach. The discrepancy model is used when interns continue to make mistakes and find it difficult to modify their behavior. When using a discrepancy model, the supervisor must be aware of its impact on trust and how the relationship with the intern will be affected. The discrepancy model should be used with caution when the intern is not performing adequately and has not responded to other strategies.

FORMATIVE AND SUMMATIVE CONFERENCES

Supervisors use two basic types of conferences with interns. In formative conferences, the intern and supervisor work together to identify effective and ineffective teaching strategies, behaviors, and attitudes. Formative conferences also involve planning and goal setting for the future. This type of conference is ongoing throughout the experience and occurs both formally and informally. Mentors should plan at least one formative conference per week, realizing that there should be informal formative discussions each day. Planning and scheduling formative conferences ensure that they take place each week.

Summative conferences are evaluative in nature. Such conferences typically occur at the midpoint and end of the clinical experience. Additional summative conferences may be necessary if an intern is not meeting the expectations of the supervisors. During the summative conference, supervisors typically share results of previous evaluations of performance and make appropriate suggestions for improvement in the future.

Formative conferences are usually more useful than summative conferences because they provide specific feedback that can be quickly implemented by an intern. These conferences are usually less formal and more loosely structured than summative conferences. When held on a regular basis, formative conferences help in omitting surprise and anxiety from the evaluation process. Honesty and openness are also encouraged by regular formative conferences.

Summative conferences make use of data from the formative conferences that have taken place and provide the intern with an evaluation of his or her performance. Formative conferences help to keep the intern informed of his or her progress throughout the assignment so that no surprises should occur at the midterm or ending evaluations of the intern.

At the beginning of the experience, formative conferences should be supervisor directed.[5] Both the mentor and university supervisor need to ensure that the intern understands the expectations for the assignment, is building positive relationships with students and staff members, and is making a positive adjustment to the classroom. During initial formative conferences, the mentor and supervisor will focus primarily on reinforcing the positive and provide remediation for any problems or concerns noticed. Positive feedback[6] builds a strong foundation for the intern's success.

Addressing and dealing with potential problems or concerns early can alleviate serious difficulties later. Supervisors should address even minor concerns immediately. Too often, supervisors assume these *little* issues will disappear, only to find out later they are a prelude to more serious concerns. Effective mentors, for example, deal with minor irritants quickly and effectively.

As the intern gains confidence and experience, the formative conference can become more of a dialogue. Clarifying and brainstorming strategies used by supervisors can encourage the intern to analyze his or her performance and suggest what has gone well and what needs further work. By the end of the clinical experience, most interns should be encouraged to lead the conference. Analyzing what has taken place in a systematic manner, determining what has gone well, and deciding how to deal with problems are key signals that professional growth has occurred. This process readies the intern for his own classroom where such decisions must be made independently.

Keeping a record of the dates and content of formative conferences provides important data, which helps make evaluation easier. A suggested form for a weekly formative conference can be found in Figure 5.1. Although at least one weekly conference is recommended, mentors may share data informally any time. Some mentors prefer to share a journal with their interns, recording observations and ideas immediately. The intern responds to the mentor's feedback in the journal, facilitating a written dialogue. This process

Figure 5.1. Weekly Conference Form

* Required

Name *

Mentor Teacher *

Date and week *

Dates tardy or absent *

Conference Agenda *

Weekly Targeted Activities *

Strengths *

Goals for Growth *

often has an unanticipated outcome—both individuals improve their ability to articulate thoughts and reflections about teaching. This outcome from journal writing usually emerges in deeper and more reflective thinking about teaching.[7]

Lesson evaluations[8] are another kind of formative data which is used to facilitate the professional growth of the intern. After reviewing an intern's plan for a lesson, the mentor observes the lesson and records ratings and feedback on a form provided by the university. A formative conference after the lesson takes place to share data with the intern and to plan for future teaching.

The records of formative conferences, along with the mentor's observations of the intern's interactions, form the basis for the summative evaluation of the intern's performance. When accurate formative records are kept, the supervisor has an invaluable reference to use when completing summative evaluations or writing reference letters for interns.

In the event that the intern is having difficulty, the formative conference records are important evidence that the intern has been provided with frequent feedback about performance. This information and record keeping is part of the due process[9] necessary if an intern is removed from a placement.

University supervisors also find formative conference records helpful. By reading the weekly summary of the discussions between mentor and intern, the university supervisor can compare the mentor's assessments of the experience with his or her own perceptions. The supervisor can easily identify areas of concern that were discussed previously. It is also recommended that the formative conference record be shared on a regular basis with the building principal. Because the principal is the instructional leader in the school, being familiar with the progress of interns assigned to the school can be helpful if parents should call about the intern or in future hiring decisions.

The summative conferences will proceed more professionally when formative conferences have been conducted and weekly records have been kept. The intern will tend to be less anxious, since there is already familiarity with issues to be discussed. The final summative conference is more likely to be a celebration of the intern's progress and end on a positive note if formative conferences have alleviated previous trouble spots. If there are serious concerns, then the intern has previously been apprised of them through formative conferences.

REINFORCING

One of the most important things a supervisor can do during the supervision process is reinforce desirable instructional behaviors. Reinforcement[10] has numerous important benefits for the intern. When reinforcement is genuine and accurate, the intern feels that the supervisor is competent, cares about her success, and that feedback given is worthwhile. Because the intern realizes that the supervisor is interested in his or her success, trust is enhanced.

When reinforcement is used effectively, an intern is able to make teaching behaviors, which may have been intuitively used, part of a conscious decision-making process in future planning and instruction. Interns are more likely to seek help from mentors and supervisors who reinforce effective behaviors than from those who utilize a discrepancy model. The most important benefit of appropriate reinforcement may be that the intern is more likely to make more frequent use of behaviors which have been reinforced, resulting in improved learning and behavior in the classroom.

Effective reinforcement of instructional behaviors results from focus, timeliness, straightforwardness, and a positive tone. Focus results from limiting the number of reinforced behaviors after a single observation. It is more productive to focus on one or two specific behaviors that can be productively used in future lessons. When a supervisor attempts to introduce too many issues, an intern may be overwhelmed with information and the feedback becomes less useful.

The value of reinforcement is lessened when too much time passes between the behavior and the reinforcement. A written note or a brief, informal conference with the intern where positive behavior is mentioned can be effective ways to provide timely reinforcement. This can be done between classes, during transition time, or during a class break.

When reinforcing, the supervisor needs to be straightforward. This means that the supervisor is genuinely reinforcing an appropriate behavior, not using reinforcement as a lead-in to unpleasant information or feedback. This last technique, though sometimes used, creates a level of mistrust and can negatively impact the mentor–intern relationship.

One problem of positive reinforcement is that some interns are not comfortable discussing what they do well. An intern may devalue the reinforcement by commenting that the behavior wasn't important, wasn't done satisfactorily, or did not take much effort. When reinforcement takes place often, and supervisors positively confront attempts to devalue efforts, interns will more likely accept reinforcement as a way to recognize quality teaching and enhance future performance.

For reinforcement to be effective in improving student achievement and attitudes in the classroom, teaching behaviors discussed must have a real effect on students in the classroom. Effective instructional behaviors that positively affect student learning can be grouped into five categories: analyzing, prescribing, determining strategies, creating effective instructional designs, and performing assessments. Observable examples of each of these categories can be found in the Appendix 2.

Analyzing behaviors involves the manner in which the intern sets goals and objectives for learning. Interns who analyze effectively make sure that appropriate state and local standards are being addressed. Appropriate diagnosis of the context in which teaching is taking place, including the diverse needs of the students, is evidence of effective instructional analysis.

Prescribing effective ways to organize learning for students requires numerous decisions. Learning activities should be clearly focused on the instructional objective for a given lesson and the objectives should be clearly understood by students. Prescribing decisions also include ways to facilitate higher-level student thinking, problem solving during instruction, and creative thinking. When prescribing instructional activities to meet the needs of diverse learners, effective interns will often utilize student groupings[11] that bring together students of varying academic achievement.

Determining appropriate instructional strategies is another category of decision making. Effective interns accommodate their students' levels and make adaptations[12] and curricular adaptions[13] for the needs of learners. Strategies are selected that help students understand and remember lessons while motivating students to become actively engaged in the learning process.

The determining appropriate strategies category also includes management decisions made by the teacher to keep students positively and productively involved. Classroom management is often one of the skills interns struggle with, especially at the beginning of their assignment. Interns should be familiar with the mentor's strategies for classroom management and use these strategies as they teach. Positive reinforcement and feedback[14] can be extremely effective strategies for the intern to use.

Effective lesson design[15] includes focusing students on learning and providing an appropriate review of what has been learned previously. Instructional input and modeling should be clear and focused. The teacher checks for understanding during the lesson and guided practice activities. Closure is provided for each instructional sequence, and appropriate independent practice is assigned.

Assessment decisions[16] take place before, during, and after instruction. Before teaching, the intern needs to determine how the students will demonstrate that they have achieved learning objectives. During instruction, checking for understanding provides information that helps adjust the pace and content of instruction as needed. After instruction, assessment provides evidence of student learning and information on which to base further instruction. How interns use assessment to evaluate their teaching will offer excellent insight for the mentor. If students do not perform well on a given assessment, the intern must reflect on each element of the instructional process to determine the reason for lack of success.

Recognizing how the intern is using effective instructional behaviors helps the mentor reinforce the intern appropriately. These five instructional decision areas, if implemented effectively, can positively impact student learning. The mentor can also work with the intern to make more frequent use of effective teaching strategies so that student learning is enhanced.

When reinforcing appropriate teaching behaviors, the mentor or university supervisor should do four things: identify, label, connect, and extend. First, the supervisor should identify the productive behavior that has been observed. This behavior should be one that has positively impacted student learning.

Next, the supervisor should label the behavior by giving it a name that the intern will recognize in later conferences. This labeling gives both parties a contextual reference for future discussions. Since many different terms for instructional behaviors exist, the intern needs to become familiar with what the supervisor is labeling as an engagement strategy, for example.

The third factor in effective reinforcement is connecting the behavior to student learning. The supervisor should tell how the behavior helped students to understand a concept or idea or how interest and motivation were facilitated.

Finally, the supervisor should, when appropriate, extend the behavior to other teaching situations by suggesting how this teaching behavior could be appropriately used in other situations. To assist the professional growth of an intern, the supervisor could ask the intern to offer suggestions of where and how this behavior could be used in the other classroom experiences. Examples of clarification questions can assist in the process.

CLARIFICATION

Clarification is the appropriate use of questioning to gain understanding and facilitate intern participation in formative and summative conferences. Benefits of clarification include improved dialog between interns and supervisors, improved understanding of decision making processes, more accurate analysis of performance, and encouragement for self-analysis by the intern.[17]

As the intern becomes more skilled and gains confidence, it is appropriate to involve him or her more in the supervisory conference. Clarification helps accomplish this by asking participants to analyze their teaching behavior. When using clarification, it is important that the supervisor listens carefully and asks follow-up questions to promote understanding. Clarification questions must seek information, not make statements or imply judgments. For example, asking if an intern was aware that four students in the back of the room were off task during a lesson is not necessarily a question but rather a

Table 5.1. Examples of Clarification Questions

1. How did you feel about the lesson you taught?
2. What things turned out well?
3. What strategies could you use when you teach again tomorrow?
4. If you were going to teach this lesson again, would you do anything differently?
5. What strategies did you use to ensure that the students understood what you were teaching?
6. How did you keep students on task during the lesson?
7. Which management strategy worked the best for you during this lesson?
8. How did you keep students engaged in the instruction?
9. How did you feel about the new strategy you tried during this lesson?
10. What did you learn from teaching this lesson?

statement of concern about management skills. Some appropriate clarification questions can be found in Table 5.1.

Clarification questions can help the supervisor understand the decision making processes the intern uses when planning, teaching, and assessing. Asking how an intern decided students were ready for the lesson, for example, assists a supervisor's understanding of how decisions about content and organization of instruction were determined. Asking about selected instructional strategies for a particular lesson lets a supervisor know how decisions are made about content and the use of teaching methods. Assessment decisions can be better understood by asking how the intern knew students understood what was being taught or why a decision was made on a particular assessment strategy for a given instructional sequence.

Clarification questions can also be used to check the intern's perceptions about students and how they reacted to a lesson. For example, asking for an analysis of class motivation or of an individual student's attentiveness helps the teacher think about what was observed while teaching. Inquiring about positive aspects of the lesson allows the supervisor to know how the intern is analyzing his or her own teaching.

Clarification strategies can help establish a positive tone during present and future conferences. At the beginning of a conference, for example, a supervisor should ask what aspects of a lesson pleased the intern. A positive statement may precede a question designed to set a positive tone. One example is, "I noticed the students were really involved in the lesson this morning. How did you get them so interested?" This question lets the intern know the supervisor noticed positive things about a lesson and encourages sharing.

After observing a lesson, if a mentor or supervisor feels students may not have understood a concept well, it may be more appropriate to clarify than give advice. If the response to a clarification question indicates an intern was aware of the problem and has planned an appropriate strategy for re-teaching the next day, then a supervisor can reinforce this decision. By using clarification in this way, the intern will be more actively involved in the supervision process and the supervisor gets a better picture of the intern's problem solving skills.

The university supervisor is less involved with the day-to-day instructional process in the classroom than the mentor teacher. During university supervisor visits, clarification helps a supervisor understand what went on in class prior to the supervisor's visit and what the intern will be doing in subsequent lessons.

University supervisors may find it helpful to ask if the lessons observed during the visit were typical for that group of students. Special circumstances of which the supervisor was unaware may have affected the students' behaviors and attitudes during the lesson. When the intern clarifies, for example, that students were uninterested in the fractions lesson because the class hamster had escaped and the students were in "hamster watch" mode, the supervisor is saved from attempting to remediate when it may not be necessary.

Sometimes, university supervisors visit when interns and their students are not at their best. When the supervisor observes or learns through clarification that the observation is not typical of what normally goes on in the classroom, the university supervisor should schedule another visit soon to observe a more representative example of teaching. This helps assure an intern that the supervisor is committed to being helpful and supportive.

During each visit, the university representative should visit with the mentor teacher to get his or her feedback on how well the assignment is going. Using clarifying questions with the mentor will assist in determining if the mentor's and intern's perceptions and reflections are similar. When perceptions are similar, usually a positive experience is taking place. If the supervisor receives mixed messages and determines that perceptions by the mentor and intern are different, it may be helpful to have a three-way conference to determine the reasons for the differing perspectives.

BRAINSTORMING

In order to meet the needs of their many diverse students, interns need to become skilled problem solvers. The ability to respond to students in new and different ways is one of the hallmarks of teacher effectiveness. Interns need encouragement from their supervisors to become critical thinkers and problem solvers. Unfortunately, mentors and university supervisors often provide answers and solutions to problems rather than encourage the intern to use creative problem-solving strategies.[18]

Brainstorming[19] provides an opportunity for the intern and supervisor to think of alternative strategies for meeting student needs in the classroom.

When an intern has been successful with students, brainstorming can be used to determine ways to build on the successful experience. Brainstorming can also be used to design alternative approaches for instruction, management, or assessment when a problem or concern has developed. Planning for future instruction is also an area in which brainstorming may be helpful. If possible, it may be helpful to involve other teachers or interns in this process. The opportunity to share and create with peers can be an excellent professional development activity.

Brainstorming usually focuses on one of three primary goals: fluency, originality, or flexibility. Fluency involves thinking of as many ideas as possible. Often, interns develop a single idea or strategy rather than exploring many. Some of the most creative ideas can come after many different ideas have been introduced, analyzed, and discussed.

Originality involves thinking of strategies that are new to the individual. For example, an intern may decide to try expanding on a strategy that has been used previously with success. The intern may also be willing to apply an approach suggested in a methods class. Originality may also involve a shift of paradigms, with new priorities becoming the focus of efforts.

Flexibility is perhaps the most challenging of the three brainstorming goals. Flexibility requires that the intern shift from old patterns of thinking and reflect in ways that may require a new thought process. Flexibility may be particularly uncomfortable since old habits of thinking and approaching problem solving may be deeply ingrained.

To utilize brainstorming effectively, the mentor or university supervisor needs to be sure sufficient time is provided. Identifying original ideas to solve challenging problems involving students is not easy, and solutions cannot be determined without a commitment of time and energy.

As with many aspects of the supervision process, the degree of trust between supervisor and intern influences the willingness to be creative and consider ideas that may seem risky. When trust is present, the intern usually feels more comfortable in suggesting ideas that may, at first glance, seem unproductive or even silly. In their own classrooms, interns will need to think creatively to solve the inevitable problems that will occur. Letting the intern participate in developing possible solutions to problems in the internship prepares the intern to accept this challenge.

Encouraging the intern to become an active participant in brainstorming and problem solving provides an opportunity for ownership of ideas that may be generated. If a mentor or supervisor suggests a solution to a problem, for example, the intern may be less committed to implementing the solution and blame the supervisor if success is not achieved.

Brainstorming requires that a supervisor help the intern become comfortable with uncertainty. There is hardly a single correct answer for most classroom challenges, and what has worked in one situation may not work in another. Interns need to understand that when a solution is unsuccessful, it does not mean failure but rather indicates an opportunity to try a variety of strategies and to demonstrate flexibility. All ideas are valuable when brainstorming, and they should be considered as future options for instruction or for solving particular problems.

Divergent questions are often the most successful technique used when brainstorming to generate a variety of options. Divergent questions are open ended. Divergent questions can help interns think about information and ideas they already know about, or have experienced, and apply that information to occurring problems. Supervisors may also use divergent questions to help an intern reflect on different strategies for solving problems in the classroom. In the event the intern is unable to think of possible alternatives, the supervisor should have several workable strategies in mind to suggest.

Convergent questions, which have only one correct answer, are not usually as helpful when brainstorming and usually limit or end discussion of new ideas. Similarly, evaluative questions, that require value judgments and can usually be answered with yes or no, also hinder the brainstorming process.

It is sometimes helpful for the supervisor to use the strategy of *hitchhiking* when brainstorming with an intern. Hitchhiking occurs when the supervisor adds information, ideas, or suggestions to the intern's responses. Hitchhiking can produce a helpful professional dialog between the supervisor and intern.

REMEDIATION

It is sometimes necessary to use part of a conference for remediation. Remediation is the process of correcting inappropriate decisions or actions and redirecting the intern to more appropriate strategies. Remediation does not need to be threatening and is a useful part of the learning process.

At the beginning of the experience, the mentor will likely use remediation to help the intern understand the mentor's expectations. Simple redirection early can avoid problems and behaviors that can become bigger issues later in the assignment. Most teachers, when establishing a classroom climate at the beginning of a new year, respond quickly to students whose behaviors do not meet their expectations. This quick response to inappropriate behaviors exhibited by an intern early in an assignment is also necessary and can alleviate potential communication problems in the future. For example, if an intern is not turning in paperwork in a timely manner or is arriving later than required, it is essential to remediate these behaviors early.

Remediation is also needed when interns use teaching and management strategies that are inappropriate or ineffective. Supervisors need to make sure interns understand the behavior or strategy that is unacceptable and why it is unacceptable. Supervisors also need to suggest a specific alternative that the intern will be expected to utilize. For example, sometimes beginning teachers respond to only a handful of students such as the brightest or most verbal while not paying attention to other students. This is an example of a concern that a mentor would share and offer positive alternatives for the intern to implement.

Remediation is most effective when the supervisor follows up with positive reinforcement as the concern is remedied or the alternative successfully employed. Unfortunately, not all problems with interns are simple ones. Interns who continue with the same areas may require more focused and intensive remediation. Working with struggling interns is discussed in Chapter 7.

It is important to provide appropriate remediation in a timely manner. The mentor teacher may hope that a particular problem will dissipate with time, but often the problem persists and the mentor becomes frustrated. Another problem with not dealing with the concerns in a timely manner is that the intern may be overwhelmed by a problem when it finally is addressed. Compounded with the frustration of a mentor, problems and concerns that are not addressed appropriately are likely to escalate and become more significant than is necessary. This is why early remediation is so important and essential.

USING TECHNOLOGY TO PROVIDE FEEDBACK TO INTERNS

The availability of email can allow the university supervisor to communicate more often with the intern and increase the amount of dialogue feedback. Some university supervisors require that the intern communicate by email at least once a week. This communication does not need to be lengthy, but should include a brief reflection on what has been accomplished during the week and what is planned for the next one. Lesson plans can also be sent to the university supervisor via email. The supervisor can analyze the lesson plans and return comments and suggestions promptly without visiting the school. If a journal is required, sharing reflections can keep the university supervisor informed. Technology allows this form of communication to occur and enhances the experience.[20]

SUMMARY

Effective supervision helps achieve the maximum benefit from the clinical experience. Mentors and university supervisors who model congruency in their interactions with intern are more successful and influential. Frequent formative conferences help promote professional growth and expertise, and when appropriately used, summative evaluation is easier and less stressful for all involved.

Supervisors need to be able to reinforce appropriate teaching behaviors and attitudes exhibited by the intern. As the intern gains skill, clarification and brainstorming may be used to facilitate more active involvement and participation by the intern in conferences. Remediation of inappropriate decisions and behaviors is most successful when concerns are identified early by the supervisor and followed up by positive reinforcement.

APPLYING WHAT YOU HAVE LEARNED

Video 5.1

In this video, https://www.youtube.com/watch?v=fruPP95DlN0, you will observe the beginning of a conference between an intern and her university supervisor. As you observe the conference, look for ways that the mentor teacher creates a positive tone during the conference. Also, look for clarifying questions that the supervisor uses to encourage the intern to actively participate during the conference.

Video 5.2

In this video, https://www.youtube.com/watch?v=f_JNuhgWgg4, you will watch a portion of a conference between a university supervisor and an intern. As you watch the conference, look for what teacher behaviors the supervisor reinforces, what clarifying questions the supervisor uses, and how the supervisor and intern brainstorm together during the conference.

NOTES

1. Lyman, L., Wilson, A., Garhart, C., Heim, M., and Winn, W. (1987). *Clinical Instruction and Supervision for Accountability.* Dubuque, Iowa: Kendall-Hunt.

2. Lyman, L., Morehead, M. A., and Foyle, H. C. (1989, Winter). "Building Teacher Trust in Supervision and Evaluation." *Illinois School Research and Development* 25(2), 55–59.

3. http://www.globoforce.com/gfblog/2014/new-research-on-performance-reviews-and-positive-feedback/

4. Lyman, L. and Foyle, H. (1990). *Cooperative Groupings for Interactive Learning: Students, Teachers, and Administrators.* Washington, DC: National Education Association, 25.

5. Jensen, J. (1998). "Supervision from Six Theoretical Frameworks." Proceedings from American Educational Research Association, San Diego, 1–34.

6. http://blog.baudville.com/give-positive-employee-feedback-with-your-own-positive-words

7. Silva, D. (2000). "Triad Journaling as a Tool for Reconceptualizing Supervision in the Professional Development School." Proceedings from American Educational Research Association, New Orleans, 1–17.

8. http://www.weber.edu/wsuimages/UCTE/Assessment/STLessonObservationForm2011.pdf

9. http://cms.bsu.edu/academics/collegesanddepartments/teachers/currentstudents/teacheredhandbook/fieldexp/termination

10. http://www.forensicmag.com/article/2013/09/using-positive-reinforcement-employee-motivation

11. https://cft.vanderbilt.edu/guides-sub-pages/setting-up-and-facilitating-group-work-using-cooperative-learning-groups-effectively/

12. http://www.edutopia.org/mi-resources

13. http://www.cgu.edu/include/Grid.of.Nine.pdf

14. http://www.edutopia.org/classroom-management-relationships-strategies-tips

15. http://www.ascd.org/publications/newsletters/education-update/oct11/vol53/num10/How-To-Plan-Effective-Lessons.aspx

16. https://www.nwea.org/blog/2015/7-ways-understand-classroom-assessments-working/

17. Lyman, L. and Foyle, H. (1989). "Creative Supervisory Conferences: New Wine in Old Skins?" *Florida ASCD Journal* 6, 45–46.

18. Lyman, L. and Foyle, H. (1989). "Creative Supervisory Conferences: New Wine in Old Skins?" *Florida ASCD Journal* 6, 45–46.

19. http://www.edudemic.com/three-techniques-brainstorming/

20. Silva, D. (2000). "Triad Journaling as a Tool for Reconceptualizing Supervision in the Professional Development School." Proceedings from American Educational Research Association, New Orleans, 1–17.

Chapter Six

Helping Interns Succeed in Diverse Classrooms

Future teachers will work in schools that are becoming increasingly diverse. Inclusion of more special-needs students in regular classrooms challenges all educators to design lessons that are appropriate for a wide range of learning abilities and styles.[1] Interns are also challenged to provide equitable learning opportunities for students so that all can be successful, regardless of socioeconomic status, language, ethnicity, gender, or ability.[2] Mentor teachers and university supervisors need to provide instructional assistance and feedback to interns so that they can be successful in today's culturally diverse[3] settings. In this chapter, a number of links are provided to strategies the mentor can suggest to interns to improve their teaching and promote more equitable practices in the classroom.

GETTING TO KNOW STUDENTS

If interns are to meet the needs of all students, the first step is becoming acquainted with the diversity in the classroom and learning about students' personalities, interests, and backgrounds. One strategy might be to conduct structured interviews with students as discussed in Chapter 2. This activity, with individual students or small groups of students, helps the intern build trust and positive relationships with children early in the experience. The mentor or university supervisor may want to provide a list of interview questions to be used in this exercise and encourage the use of questions provided while conducting the interviews. Possible interview questions can be found in Table 2.2. The intern can make notes of useful information about each student and will sometimes discover information about students of which the mentor is unaware.

As discussed in Chapter 4, guided observation[4] of the class can help an intern become acquainted with the students and provide an opportunity to check the accuracy of his perceptions about students. If inaccuracies or biases are evident, the mentor can assist the intern in developing a more accurate and tolerant view of students. Discussing the guided observation with the intern can also help the mentor to check the intern's understanding of classroom rules and procedures and the mentor's classroom management strategies.

In the first few days of the experience, the mentor and intern should discuss the makeup of the class. Gender, economic factors, and ethnic demographics can be reviewed together. Even with the emphasis on multicultural themes in teacher education programs, interns may not be aware of situations that are particular to the region, district, or school. Mentors should alert interns about taboos that exist because of cultural factors or school and district regulations. For example, in science, performing experiments with certain animals may not be acceptable. In art, depicting certain individuals or animals in a particular manner may not be appropriate in the area or district. Even the celebration of the Christmas holiday in many areas is prohibited or limited to very specific activities. Making interns aware of these issues early will keep them from making serious mistakes that would offend some in the community and in the class.

Interns who participate in the beginning of the school year have opportunities to observe how the teacher uses group-building activities[5] to create a community in the classroom. These activities provide opportunities for all students to develop an appreciation for individual differences and encourage students to view each other and the teacher as members of the classroom community. Such activities are necessary at the beginning of the school year and throughout the year in order to sustain successful collaboration among students.[6] An example of a group-building activity can be found in Table 6.1.

Table 6.1. Sample Group Building Activity

This group-building activity would be suitable for students in a secondary social studies class.
People Search
Find someone who can sign each box. Each box must have a different signature.

Find someone who can tell you the first sentence of the Gettysburg Address.	Find someone who can tell you what two words were added to the Pledge of Allegiance during the 1950s.	Find someone who can tell you the address of the White House on Pennsylvania Avenue in Washington, DC.	Find someone who can tell you the approximate population of the world.
Find someone who can whistle or hum a patriotic song.	Find someone who can play a musical instrument.	Find someone who can tell you whose picture is on the $5 bill.	Find someone who likes to dance.

Table 6.1 *(continued)*

Find someone who took pictures of a trip they took last summer.	Find someone who can name the Vice President of the United States.	Find someone who worked on a committee in the past where the members worked well together.	Find someone who has written a letter to a newspaper.
Find someone who has kept a diary or journal sometime in their life.	Find someone who can name an extinct animal.	Find someone who can tell you when the next full moon will occur.	Find someone who comes from a family of four or more children.

Source: Adapted from Lyman, L. and Foyle, H. (1999). "Lessons Learned from a Multiculturally, Economically Diverse Classroom Setting." Proceedings from the 79th annual conference, National Council for the Social Studies. Orlando, Florida.

When the intern observes students interacting during group-building activities, important information about interpersonal skills of students, academic strengths and weaknesses, and cliques that may try to dominate activities can be determined. This information can be valuable to the intern while planning to meet the needs of all students, especially if cooperative learning groups are used.

PROMOTING EQUITABLE TEACHING PRACTICES

Providing students with equitable opportunities[7] for involvement and success should be a goal of every teacher. Supervisors can provide valuable feedback to enhance the intern's awareness of practices they use that encourage or discourage student involvement and success.

If students are to be involved and successful while the intern is working with them, they must be accorded opportunities for participation and given positive feedback about their accomplishments. As the intern begins to reach whole-group lessons, the mentor and supervisor should observe instructional sequences and record data about interactions with students. Initially, the mentor and university supervisor will want to observe the intern's interaction patterns with students. Data can be gathered by using a copy of the class seating chart. During a class discussion, for example, a mark can be made on the seating chart as students are called upon. This coding of observational data can be shared with the intern during formative conferences to encourage the intern to provide opportunities for involvement and success for all students.

While moving about the classroom, a mark on the seating chart can be made when the intern stops to help or interact with a student. Interactions with students[8] at the beginning of class, during passing periods, and at the end of class can also be recorded. The goal of these observations is to provide the intern with information about which students are receiving attention and which students are not. During the formative conference, this information can be shared to help identify students who are not involved and to better reflect on the intern's interactions with students.

Students also need equitable opportunities to experience success in the classroom. A seating chart can again be used to record interactions between the intern and students. When noting successful opportunities, the mentor or university supervisor records a "+" on the seating chart when a student answers a question correctly or receives feedback that is positive. If a student is unsuccessful or negative feedback is given, the "–" symbol can be used. If the student is initially unsuccessful, but a prompt from the teacher results in a successful response from the student, the "+" symbol would follow the "–" symbol. This indicates the intern helped the student succeed with teacher assistance. This may seem a bit confusing, but after a couple of class observations, the coding process will become easy.

As the intern begins taking over more of the instruction in the classroom, the mentor or supervisor can provide additional feedback about the kinds of response opportunities being offered to students. While observing a lesson in which the intern is using questioning during a class discussion, the mentor teacher or university supervisor can make a list of the questions asked and to whom.

During formative conferences, the mentor or supervisor helps the intern analyze questions asked during the lesson. Questions that promote recall or lower-level cognitive responses are identified. Questions that encourage higher-level cognition, problem solving, or creativity are also noted. The mentor or university supervisor then helps the intern analyze which students were asked higher-level questions.[9] The goal for the intern is to be aware that all students need opportunities for critical and creative thinking. As the intern matures professionally, the mentor may request that the intern do the same coding of observational data while the mentor teaches. This guided observation will enhance dialogue and allow the mentor to observe the depth of understanding about teaching by the intern.

As the intern begins to check students' work, the mentor should review work that has been corrected. The first concern is to ensure that the intern has been accurate in his assessment of student work. Important in this process is consideration for varying student academic abilities, strengths, and limitations. The mentor should encourage the intern to notice something positive about the work of each student.[10] As the mentor looks though corrected work, she should note when positive comments have been made.

This practice should be encouraged and interns should make positive comments[11] on as many papers as possible when assessing students' work. This strategy enables students to recognize their own success and encourages them to use similar strategies in future assignments. Assessment strategies must be multiple in nature and include a variety of techniques. It is no longer acceptable to utilize only paper-and-pencil forms of assessment. Most interns have been introduced to multiple assessment techniques during their preservice program. Mentors should encourage them to use a variety of these assessment strategies in planning and teaching.

PLANNING FOR DIVERSITY

As the intern plans for instruction, the mentor will typically be involved in making sure instructional plans are appropriate for the needs, interests, and developmental levels of a diverse student population. To meet the needs of a wide range of learners, interns need to adapt and modify instructional outcomes. Adapting instructional tasks for differing abilities is necessary so all students can feel successful and challenged by the curriculum. When students are asked to perform too difficult or easy tasks, frustration and management problems can result.[12]

Interns should be encouraged to plan appropriate lessons and learning activities for the needs of students by including adaptations[13] as part of their planning and implementation. For example, students who are highly motivated may be given modified questions and asked to assist another when finished; some may need more time, increased support, or modified instruction to be successful. Interns may also need to adapt the difficulty level of the learning task for the student or vary the way in which the student demonstrates success.[14] This can be accomplished by the way in which students are assessed. Table 6.2 offers a list of assessment strategies.

Table 6.2. Some Ways to Assess Student Performance

1. Teacher observations
2. Student verbal response
3. Portfolios
4. Cooperative activities
5. Written assignments
6. Testing
7. Hands-on activities
8. Oral analysis of topic
9. Written analysis of topic
10. Art activities related to topic
11. Physical representation developed by student
12. Role-playing

USING A VARIETY OF TEACHING STRATEGIES

In order to meet the needs of diverse students, interns must be encouraged to use a variety of instructional strategies and practices. No one way of teaching can be expected to work for all students.[15] A common problem for interns at the secondary level, for example, is the lack of modeling and limited use of numerous instructional strategies.

Howard Gardner has identified eight different intelligence areas that can be identified in students who are present in today's schools.[16] As beginners in the classroom, however, many interns limit their teaching to one or two intelligence areas, often concentrating on the verbal and mathematical forms.

Mentors can assist by identifying strategies that meet diverse student needs by using a variety of activities designed to appeal to different intelligence areas.[17] For instruction to be successful with all students, it must be designed to link to the learning strengths and intelligence areas of students.[18]

Interns often utilize paper-and-pencil tasks that require the use of verbal intelligence. It is also important for interns to provide opportunities for students to communicate with others in the classroom, thereby using and improving language skills. Since the primary purpose of acquiring language skills is to communicate with others effectively, students need opportunities to communicate with each other, learn about each other, resolve differences, and solve learning problems cooperatively.[19]

The overuse of written activities may place the second language learners at a disadvantage in the classroom. Interns must be encouraged to support the learning of second language learners through activities that allow them to practice language skills in nonthreatening and authentic ways.[20] Puppet shows, role-playing, and student-produced news shows are just a few ways to involve students who are acquiring new language skills. These examples of nonthreatening strategies will enhance the learning atmosphere of a classroom for all students.[21]

Logical intelligence can be useful in helping students become critical and creative thinkers.[22] Interns should plan activities that encourage students to use problem-solving skills and metacognition as critical thinkers.[23] Interns also need to encourage students to approach learning tasks creatively. Activities that move beyond basic skills and factual information can encourage students to generate ideas they might not think of otherwise.[24]

Mentors should encourage the use of movement activities that complement the body-kinesthetic intelligence to assist in meeting diverse learners' needs. In all grades, but especially in the early elementary experience, students have a particular need for learning activities that incorporate movement. These activities can be integrated with other intelligence areas to involve students in developmentally appropriate learning experiences.[25]

Mentors should help the interns monitor students' nonverbal cues to determine when a break is needed. At the elementary level, one strategy that may be useful for interns to use is brain breaks.[26] At the secondary level, a teacher can use transition times or modify seating during a class period to enhance active participation. Interns can get additional ideas for incorporating appropriate body-kinesthetic activities from the physical education teacher or others in the school who use physical learning activities in their curriculum.

Integrating music in lessons should be encouraged and may be used to relax students when entering the class or as background music for study. Some teachers may find a rhythmic clapping pattern a useful strategy for gaining student attention. Harry Wong describes several activities that utilize rhythm or pattering.[27] Both musical and movement[28] activities can enhance the learning opportunities for all students and increase the instructional techniques available to the intern. Using music or physical activities that are part of other cultures validates the culture and demonstrates a teacher's respect for it.

Pictures, diagrams, charts, and graphic organizers complement the visual intelligence area of students. Interns should be encouraged to incorporate visual strategies into their lessons frequently, especially with younger learners. Technology[29] can be used creatively to support visual learning. Pictures from students' cultures will enhance the feeling of belonging and create an atmosphere where students can relate to the content.

Interns should also be alert to the physical appearance of the classroom. Is student work on display? If so, does the work represent all students in the class? To increase student interest and involvement, interns can take snapshots of students as they are engaged in learning activities and display them. Displaying work[30] from every student indicates that the teacher respects the diversity of the students and values them as individuals. Art teachers can provide interns with other ideas for integrating visual activities into their teaching. Allowing time to visit other classes and noting the things teachers display in their rooms can be helpful for interns.

CULTURE

Helping students learn to interact and communicate effectively with people from a variety of cultures is an important skill needed for success in and outside of the classroom. Interns should be encouraged to incorporate cooperative learning[31] activities into lessons to promote involvement and build interpersonal skills for all students. Group-building activities[32] can provide opportunities for diverse students to cooperate and build a classroom community. For example, the use of class meetings can encourage group communication and problem solving when difficulties arise in the classroom. When conducting these meetings, the intern should monitor student interaction and make sure ethnically diverse students have an opportunity for input. Counselors can provide strategies for helping manage student conflict, teaching social skills, enhancing interpersonal skills, and balancing gender interactions.

Interns should provide ethnically diverse students opportunities to develop self-awareness and confidence. De-emphasizing the importance of external evaluation tools and encouraging students to reflect on their own progress and effort should also be a part of the experience. During a time of accountability and standardized testing,[33] some students feel they are inadequate and a failure because of their test scores.

This is especially true for many second language learners and those from lower socioeconomic situations. It is essential that interns understand the impact these scores can have on students and their perception of future expectations and success. Educators should communicate that standardized test scores are just one small piece of information about a student and are not indicative of overall intelligence or potential for success.

Reflection journals can provide all students with an opportunity to personalize learning and think about how learning is important. Portfolios maintained by students provide documentation of learning and allow educators to assess student performance in multiple ways. Journals and portfolios are important elements in classrooms that meet the needs of diverse learners. These materials can also be learning tools for the intern. Personal reflection[34] is also important for interns and can provide direction for the intern's professional growth.

BIAS

Bias takes on many forms and can occur between students, and between teachers and students. In the classroom, bias can happen in textbooks, online resources, standardized tests, and in class instruction. Interns today have been made aware of multicultural issues and biases that emerge in obvious and subtle ways it is important for interns to observe how these issues impact learning and interaction in real classroom settings.

Assisting the intern in identifying bias[35] in books, online resources, curriculum, and in instruction is essential to their future success. As the relationship between mentor and intern matures and trust is secured, the mentor and intern should attempt to identify sources of bias in their teaching.

Most teachers feel they are free of bias and some express this by saying, "I treat all students equally" or "I do not see color in my classroom." Those statements will be warning to an intern or visiting supervisor who is well versed in multicultural themes. Excellent teachers and truly unbiased educators will treat children differently. What they really do is respect[36] the child's culture and language and value each student's background. Excellent teachers also realize that students have different abilities and meet those needs by varying instruction, assignments, and assessment strategies.

ASSESSMENT

Varying assessment techniques[37] is part of any excellent teacher's approach in the classroom. Interns must be aware of numerous techniques and be able to integrate those within the instructional process. In order to meet the learning styles or cultural needs of students, a teacher must vary how learning is assessed. Mentor teachers should model how they assess student learning and allow the intern to visit other teachers who approach assessment differently. Establishing a successful classroom requires the use of multiple forms of assessment and allows students with different language skills the opportunity to succeed. Paper-and-pencil assessment should be a part of any plan but must not be the sole manner in which a teacher assesses student learning.

Finally, like so many other issues related to teaching, the intern and supervisors must discuss at length cultural, language, bias, and assessment issues throughout the experience. Ignoring these will not give an intern a true opportunity for future success. Zimpher and Ashburn point out the importance of discussing cultural issues and the challenges teachers face each day.[38] These discussions should be ongoing and should be conducted in both written and oral forms. As the intern progresses through the experience, the focus will move from "What should I be doing?" to "What do the students need?" Once this transition takes place, the intern has taken a major step toward becoming a teacher.

CREATING MEANING

Mentors and university supervisors should encourage interns to find ways to make learning meaningful[39] for all students. As we know, relating the content of lessons to the needs, interests, and cultures of students can increase involvement and reduce management problems. Authentic learning tasks encourage student involvement and help make learning meaningful. Interns should develop learning around tasks that are related to real-life experiences and situations that reflect and value the cultures represented in the class.

Zeichner describes the need for high expectations for all students and the use of scaffolding that relates home and cultural experiences to school.

Zeichner points out that school customs and expectations must be addressed and that students from diverse backgrounds need to be cognizant of these in order to succeed. Therefore, part of an intern's experience must include the opportunity to instruct students in the customs of schooling. Additionally, high expectations and supporting academic experiences with cultural foundations of the student also enhance opportunities for success. Mentor teachers must ensure that interns approach all students with these expectations.[40]

MANAGEMENT

Classroom management in diverse settings is the key to success for the intern. Supervisors need to ensure discipline strategies[41] utilized by interns are appropriate for student developmental levels and that students are not embarrassed or humiliated. Understanding how students from different cultures react to teacher supervision is important information for an intern. Treating students with respect, being nonthreatening, and giving students options will increase an intern's opportunity for success with all students. It is especially important to understand how respect is demonstrated in certain cultures. For example, many teachers expect a student to look at them when discussing a discipline situation, but in some cultures, that is a sign of disrespect. Alerting an intern to this type of cultural behavior will assist the intern when interacting with students.

Additionally, if the intern follows the procedures and regulations of the mentor, the transition will be smoother when assuming full responsibility for the classroom. If the intern attempts to stray from already established rules and procedures, a disconnect will occur with students and the transition will be very difficult. As the intern assumes increased responsibility for teaching in the classroom, the mentor should monitor management of the classroom to ensure that positive reinforcement and feedback[42] is being given to all students. Mentors should reinforce examples of the intern's use of positive reinforcement, especially early in the assignment. Examples from an intern's lesson can be found in Table 6.3.

When students' inappropriate behaviors need to be addressed, the mentor needs to ensure that corrections are implemented without favoritism and in a nonthreatening manner. Nonthreatening behaviors demonstrated by the intern could include, but are not limited to, speaking in a softer voice, slowing pace of speech, tone of voice, awareness of nonverbal and facial cues, and meeting privately with the student.

The mentor teacher also needs to be certain that the intern is aware of situations in the classroom in which students may feel threatened. Since bullying[43] and harassment are inappropriate behaviors, the mentor needs to make sure the intern acts proactively to deal with these issues. Inappropriate use of

Table 6.3. Examples of Positive Reinforcement and Feedback from an Intern's Lesson

Almost everyone is in their seats ready to go.
_____ is sitting nice and quietly.
I like how _____ is reading quietly.
Thanks, _____, for being ready to listen.
Very good
_____'s hand was up really fast, we'll wait for others.
Good job
Perfect
Awesome, you're getting very quick at this.
That's a great example.
Two people have already found it.
_____ has put her name on her paper.
_____ and _____ are off to a great start.
I like how _____ is working without his voice.

put downs, sarcasm, or threats[44] by the intern should be noted and stopped immediately. Because of the diversity of the student population, these behaviors are not appropriate for the classroom and may be interpreted as offensive to students. Teachers who utilize these behaviors have a negative effect on students with often serious, unknown consequences. If this behavior is not corrected immediately, the entire experience is in jeopardy.

As discussed in Chapter 5, interns should utilize the mentor teacher's style of classroom management and follow the rules and procedures the mentor has established for the classroom. As the intern gains skill and confidence, he or she can be encouraged to try different management strategies. One of the most important goals of a successful clinical experience is for the intern to leave the experience feeling confident in his or her ability to manage the classroom so that learning and interactions are positive and productive.

THE MENTOR TEACHER AS MODEL

The mentor is the professional model with whom the intern will have the most contact during the clinical experience and is one who will have and can have a strong, positive affect on the intern's professional growth and development. Mentors must demonstrate equitable treatment of students when planning, teaching, and assessing. Interns will need advice on students and their background, but the timing, context, and tone of the information provided by the mentor can have a dramatic impact on the intern's perception and expectations for students. It is important for the mentor teacher to help the intern clarify their perceptions about students and to provide feedback on how well the intern's teaching decisions and behaviors are impacting the learning of all students. It is also important for the mentor to encourage the intern to reflect on these issues.

SUMMARY

Diverse classrooms can present considerable challenges for future teachers. Opportunities to get acquainted with students, communities, and families help interns learn about the children they will teach. Monitoring instruction

Table 6.4. Observable Teaching Behaviors That Are Effective in Diverse Classrooms

The following suggestions were gathered by groups of mentor teachers working on a grant sponsored by the Kansas Department of Education at Emporia State University in July, 2001. What ideas can you and your intern add to the list?

1. Are interns adjusting lessons to meet the needs of all students?
2. Are interns choosing materials for teaching that are appropriate to the interests and developmental levels of students?
3. Are interns varying their instructional strategies to meet the needs and developmental levels of students?
4. Are interns selecting varying assessments that meet the needs and developmental levels of students?
5. Do interns promote a nonthreatening classroom environment?
6. Do interns provide opportunities for all students to respond?
7. Do interns give positive reinforcement equitably to students?
8. Do cooperative learning groups encourage all students to work together?
9. Do interns adapt teaching and assessments to meet the needs of all students?
10. Do interns ask challenging questions of all students?
11. Do the interns' lesson plans reflect preparation to meet the needs of all students?
12. Do interns celebrate other cultures?
13. Do interns notice appropriate strategies the mentor teacher uses for working with diverse students and apply these strategies in their own teaching?
14. Do interns videotape the students while they are teaching to observe student behavior and involvement?
15. Are the grading procedures used by the intern fair?
16. Does the intern encourage the ESL student to teach him or her a few words of the student's own language?
17. Does the intern incorporate different multiple intelligence activities into lesson planning?
18. What do students in the class say about the intern?
19. Read the intern's reflections to determine how they view the students.
20. Does the intern move around the room while teaching?
21. Does the intern communicate with parents and have communications translated into the parents' languages?

and interactions with students to ensure that the intern is using equitable teaching practices, adapting instruction appropriately so all students can be successful, using a variety of teaching strategies, and making material meaningful for students provide the mentor and supervisor with data to foster professional growth of the intern and to improve teaching effectiveness. By observing and monitoring effective teaching behaviors in diverse classrooms, supervisors can ensure positive teaching experiences for interns in today's multicultural school settings. Table 6.4 provides observable teaching behaviors that can assist supervisors when working with future teachers. Supervisors and mentors need to be aware of bias and help the intern to deal equitably with all students.

APPLYING WHAT YOU HAVE LEARNED

Video 6.1

In this video, https://www.youtube.com/watch?v=A_AhAki_JEc, you will observe an intern struggling with the diverse students in his classroom. What advice would you give this intern about how to help his students be successful?

Video 6.2

In this video, https://www.youtube.com/watch?v=6CgYiA0NNlI, you will observe a conference between a supervisor and an intern. What strategies are identified from the intern's reflection and the supervisor's reinforcement that are effective in meeting the learning needs of the diverse students in the intern's classroom?

ADDITIONAL RESOURCES FOR INTERNS, MENTORS, AND UNIVERSITY SUPERVISORS

Classroom Management

https://sites.google.com/site/corkysconnections/

Group Building	https://sites.google.com/site/creatingclassroomcommunities/communities
Cooperative Learning	https://sites.google.com/site/creatingclassroomcommunities/strategies

NOTES

1. Azwell, T. S., Foyle, H. C., Lyman, L., and Smith, N. L. (1999). *Constructing Curriculum in Context*. Dubuque, Iowa: Kendall-Hunt.
2. Azwell, T. S., Foyle, H. C., Lyman, L., and Smith, N. L. (1999). *Constructing Curriculum in Context*. Dubuque, Iowa: Kendall-Hunt.
3. http://www.edutopia.org/blog/preparing-cultural-diversity-resources-teachers
4. http://www.nhcs.net/humanresources/Beginning%20Teacher%20Support%20Program/Guided_Observationform.pdf
5. http://eric.ed.gov/?id=EJ578622
6. Lyman, L. and Foyle, H. (1990). *Cooperative Groupings for Interactive Learning: Students, Teachers, and Administrators*. Washington, DC: National Education Association, 16–17.
7. http://laspdg.org/files/Equitable%20Classroom%20Practices%20Observation%20Checklist.pdf
8. http://www.eirc.org/wp-content/uploads/2015/11/TESA-Cheat-Sheet-For-Teachers.pdf
9. http://www.readwritethink.org/parent-afterschool-resources/tips-howtos/encourage-higher-order-thinking-30624.html
10. Azwell, T. S., Foyle, H. C., Lyman, L., and Smith, N. L. (1999). *Constructing Curriculum in Context*. Dubuque, Iowa: Kendall-Hunt.
11. https://www.teachingchannel.org/blog/2014/07/23/alternatives-to-the-word-great/
12. Azwell, T. S., Foyle, H. C., Lyman, L., and Smith, N. L. (1999). *Constructing Curriculum in Context*. Dubuque, Iowa: Kendall-Hunt.
13. http://www.khps.org/files/8613/9100/2965/classroom_adaptations1_20121127_152737_3.pdf
14. Deschenes, C., Ebeling, D., and Sprague, J. (1999). *Adapting Curriculum and Instruction in Inclusive Classrooms: A Teacher's Desk Reference*. Bloomington, Ind.: Center for School and Community Integration, Indiana University, 18–19.
15. Obiakor, F. E. (1994). *The Eight-Step Multicultural Approach: Teaching and Learning with a Smile*. Dubuque, Iowa: Kendall/Hunt, 46–54.
16. Gardner, H. (1983). *Frames of Mind: The Theory of Multiple Intelligences*. New York: Basic Books, 73–276.
17. http://www.edutopia.org/multiple-intelligences-research
18. Azwell, T. S., Foyle, H. C., Lyman, L., and Smith, N. L. (1999). *Constructing Curriculum in Context*. Dubuque, Iowa: Kendall-Hunt.
19. Lyman, L., Foyle, H. C., and Azwell, T. S. (1993). *Cooperative Learning in the Elementary Classroom*. Washington, DC: National Education Association, 98–99.
20. http://www.ascd.org/ascd-express/vol5/511-breiseth.aspx
21. Delpit, L. (1998). *Language Diversity and Learning in Beyond Heroes and Holidays*. Washington, DC: Network of Educators on the Americas.
22. Delpit, L. (1998). *Language Diversity and Learning in Beyond Heroes and Holidays*. Washington, DC: Network of Educators on the Americas.

23. Lyman, L., Foyle, H. C., and Azwell, T. S. (1993). *Cooperative Learning in the Elementary Classroom*. Washington, DC: National Education Association, 98–99.

24. Stinson, W., Mehroff, J. H., and Thies, S. A. (1993). *Quality Thematic Lesson Plans for Classroom Teachers: Movement Activities for Pre-K and Kindergarten*. Dubuque, Iowa: Kendall/Hunt.

25. Azwell, T. S., Foyle, H. C., Lyman, L., and Smith, N. L. (1999). *Constructing Curriculum in Context*. Dubuque, Iowa: Kendall-Hunt.

26. http://www.edutopia.org/blog/brain-breaks-focused-attention-practices-lori-desautels

27. Wong, H. K. and Wong, R. T. (1998). *How to Be an Effective Teacher the First Days of School*. Mountain View, Calif.: Harry K. Wong Publications, 176–177.

28. http://www.education.com/reference/article/four-important-reasons-including-music/

29. http://diwithtech.blogspot.com/2011/02/technology-and-visual-learner.html

30. https://www.responsiveclassroom.org/displaying-student-work/

31. http://www.learnnc.org/lp/pages/4653

32. http://www.nssa.us/journals/2010-33-2/pdf/33-2%2013%20Lyman.pdf

33. http://fairtest.org/how-standardized-testing-damages-education-pdf

34. http://www.edutopia.org/discussion/value-reflective-practice-schools

35. http://neatoday.org/2015/09/09/when-implicit-bias-shapes-teacher-expectations/

36. http://beyondpenguins.ehe.osu.edu/issue/polar-plants/creating-an-equitable-classroom-through-establishing-respect

37. http://www.edutopia.org/assessment-guide-description

38. Zimpher, N. and Ashburn, E. (1992). "Counteracting Parochialism in Teacher Candidates." In *Diversity in Teacher Education*, edited by M. Dilworth. San Francisco: Jossey-Bass, 40–62.

39. http://www.edutopia.org/blog/making-learning-meaningful-and-lasting-david-cutler

40. Zeichner, K., Melnick, S., and Gomez, M. L. (1996). *Currents of Reform in Pre-service Teacher Education*. New York: Teachers College Press, 109–176.

41. http://www.educationworld.com/a_admin/admin/admin534.shtml

42. https://my.vanderbilt.edu/specialeducationinduction/files/2013/07/Tip-Sheet-Positive-Reinforcement-Strategies.pdf

43. http://www.tolerance.org/supplement/bullying-guidelines-teachers

44. http://susanfitzell.com/articles-by-susan-fitzell/best-practice-establish-a-no-putdown-rule-in-your-classroom/

Chapter Seven

The Struggling Intern

Working with an intern who is experiencing problems in the classroom is a concern of most mentor teachers and university supervisors. By identifying the reasons why the intern is struggling and formulating appropriate plans for remediation, mentors and supervisors can maximize the possibilities for success of interns who have difficulty meeting the expectations of their assignments.

WHAT IS A STRUGGLING INTERN?

A struggling intern lacks skills and attitudes that are essential for success in the classroom. Most interns display some minor difficulties in one or two areas during the experience. These problems are usually short term concerns and are easily remediated with normal supervision. Interns who demonstrate short term concerns or isolated areas of concern are usually able to complete their assignments with success when provided with appropriate assistance.

Caruso outlines six stages of development for interns. Phase 2 of the stages is identified as confusion/clarity. While excellent interns move through all six stages very quickly, the struggling intern progresses much more slowly and may never pass the *confusion* of Phase 2.[1]

Mentor teachers and university supervisors can identify struggling interns through their observations and interactions with the intern. For example, struggling interns may demonstrate poor planning, ineffective interpersonal skills, and weak classroom management.

When an intern is struggling, the learning of students in the classroom is negatively impacted, so it is important to provide remediation to help the intern perform more effectively. It is essential that the areas of weakness and remediation efforts be documented by the mentor and supervisor.

The goal of the mentors and supervisors is to provide the necessary assistance so that interns can be successful. However, it is important to remember that not all interns can or should be "saved." The failure of an intern who has received appropriate remediation but does not make the required progress is not the fault of the mentor or the university supervisor. Ultimate responsibility for success rests with the intern. This statement is very important to remember, since most mentor teachers feel the failure of an intern is their fault.

When working with a struggling intern with serious concerns, most mentors and supervisors will spend countless hours working to improve an intern's performance. Unfortunately, some interns are unable to internalize and effectively put into practice recommendations made by supervisors.

It is always difficult for caring mentors and supervisors to inform an intern who has invested considerable time, effort, and expense to become a teacher that he or she is not succeeding in the clinical experience. Supervisors need to remember that their primary concern needs to be the learning and welfare of the intern's future students. With serious teacher shortages in the United States, it is possible that districts will be forced to hire less than ideal candidates to fill empty classrooms. Documentation of the intern's progress during the clinical experience, including remediation efforts provided, are crucial in making sure that struggling interns do not become licensed teachers without first demonstrating the necessary skills and attitudes for success. A good question to ask when determining competence is, "Would I want this individual teaching my child or grandchild next year?"

Three general causes can be identified for why interns struggle.[2] First, interns may be unskilled. Second, an intern may be unaware. Lastly, if efforts to remediate interns who are unskilled or unaware are unsuccessful, the intern may be unable or unwilling to work productively with students in the classroom as a teacher.

THE UNSKILLED INTERN

It is common at the beginning of the clinical experience for an intern to demonstrate less than proficient skills and abilities. After all, the intern is in the mentor's classroom to acquire and enhance the skills needed for successful teaching. One of the most important factors in whether an unskilled intern will be able to be successful is dispositional: the willingness of the unskilled intern to accept and implement recommendations for improvement. With an intern who is willing, an improvement plan[3] can usually be developed that assists the intern in acquiring the necessary skills to be successful.

When working with an unskilled intern, supervisors should provide examples from the intern's work that demonstrate a need for improvement[4] and professional growth. For example, if an intern is not dealing with student off-task behavior appropriately, specific examples of these behaviors should be identified. To make the intern aware that supervisors are concerned, examples should be discussed, and specific descriptions of the students' activities should be shared.

After providing examples of the areas that need improvement, mentors and supervisors can effectively coach[5] struggling interns by providing specific strategies for the interns to try in future lessons. If the intern is able to apply the suggestions effectively, the mentor and supervisor can reinforce both the intern's developing skills and the intern's effort to improve.

When working with an unskilled intern, it is usually helpful to address one area of concern at a time. By focusing on a single, specific area of concern, an intern can concentrate on efforts of improvement. It is easier for supervisors to give specific feedback when focusing on only one area of improvement. Also, if the intern experiences success in dealing with one area of concern, it becomes easier to target other areas because his confidence has been elevated.

Most unskilled interns are aware of their own shortcomings but do not know how to solve the problems. A helpful strategy in identifying solutions is to allow the intern to observe the mentor[6] and look for specific ways in which he or she deals with similar classroom situations. Requiring taking notes while observing ensures that the intern is correctly identifying workable strategies that the mentor is using.

It may also be helpful for the intern to observe another teacher in the school who is very successful in working with problematic areas that have been identified. A conference with the teacher to be observed is not only courteous, professional practice but also allows the colleague to make sure strategies are demonstrated that would be helpful to the intern.

Another possibility is for the intern to observe the university supervisor or principal as he or she teaches a demonstration lesson with the students in the classroom. Many different approaches to teaching exist, and it will usually be helpful for the interns to become acquainted with a number of approaches to address specific problems or concerns they may be having.

After the intern has had the opportunity to watch other professionals, a plan for improvement should be developed with the active involvement of the intern. During a planning conference, the intern should be able if asked to identify those strategies observed during other classroom visits. The supervisors should also identify strategies that they believe would work well for the intern. After these steps, the supervisors should help the intern incorporate the strategies into planning and implementation.

When working with an unskilled intern, the number of formative conferences will increase. Although it is usually appropriate to have a brief formative conference at least once a week, a daily conference should be held, if possible, while the intern is working on an improvement plan. Feedback should be specific and directed to the areas of concern which were identified. Both mentors and university supervisors need to note specific examples of progress and encourage the intern to continue utilizing strategies that are working well.

Unskilled interns need reassurance that all teachers struggle from time to time. Supervisors need to emphasize that teachers will encounter problems that need to be addressed throughout their careers. The intern's reflective practice[7] will ideally continue throughout the intern's career. Interns should also be encouraged to seek assistance from colleagues throughout their career.

Unfortunately, there are a few struggling interns who blame others for problems they are having. For example, the intern may tell the mentor, "They did not teach us that at the university." The blame may also be directed toward the attitudes of the children in the classroom or the mentor teacher. Life situations such as family, work, or illness may also be offered as excuses.

Mentors and supervisors need to redirect the blaming intern to focus on the expectations which are not being met and to commit the time and energy required to make needed changes. The intern who is not able to do this may be unable or unwilling to make the improvements needed to be successful.

THE UNAWARE INTERN

Interns may display incompetence without being aware that there is a problem. In response to clarification questions, for example, an intern may indicate that a lesson went well when, in fact, the mentor had several concerns about it. An intern may be in denial or really not know that something is wrong. Lack of awareness often manifests itself early in the experience and should be a red flag to supervisors. This type of intern should receive remediation early in the experience. Helping the intern to be aware of how his or her teaching impacts students should be the focus of supervision.

Like the unskilled interns, those who are unaware need to be given specific examples of areas of concern. Awareness that a problem exists is increased when both supervisors refer to the standards reflected in procedures or evaluations. The mentor and university supervisor should compare the performance of and expectations for interns and make sure it is understood why improvement is needed.

The unaware intern may become defensive, suggesting that the areas of concern are not problems. For example, sometimes individuals will state that the teaching strategies they used are similar to the ones they experienced in elementary school. To counter this argument, supervisors can discuss the many changes in students, curriculum standards, technology, and student diversity that make different strategies necessary. Most interns, once aware that there are concerns about performance, are eager to improve.

As they become more aware of the need to improve, an intern usually exhibits the characteristics and attitudes of an unskilled intern, and procedures for assisting them are similar to those of the unskilled intern. Those techniques are observing others, addressing one concern at a time, offering specific feedback, and formulating an improvement plan.

Interns who are unaware they have problems may become unduly concerned about their progress when weaknesses are identified and discussed. Mentors and university supervisors should be positive and supportive during this initial phase. Noticing and commenting on specific improvements and efforts made by the intern to improve usually reassures and encourages the intern. Frequent, focused feedback, identifying improvements, and encouraging the intern to continue to work on areas that still need improvement are key components when working with interns who are actively working to improve their teaching skills.

Unskilled or unaware interns can provide helpful data for analyzing the teacher education program to determine if the deficiencies of the intern are partially a result of not being taught the necessary information, not having sufficient opportunities to practice needed skills, or not being able to reflect effectively on performance and make needed changes. Mentors and supervisors can use this information to recommend changes or additions to the program of study and experiences that interns have before the clinical experience takes place.

THE UNABLE OR UNWILLING INTERN

Although most problems experienced by interns can be remediated successfully using the processes described, a few interns will not make the improvements that are necessary. In most cases, either the intern who continues to struggle after appropriate remediation has occurred is unable to develop the appropriate skills needed or is unwilling to make necessary changes. It may be possible to help the unable or unwilling intern who continues to struggle, but a great deal of effort is required to do so.

When remediation efforts have been unsuccessful, the mentor needs to communicate concerns to the university supervisor as soon as possible. If the supervisor has not already been involved in the improvement process, he or she must be included immediately. The earlier a university representative becomes a participant, the more likely all due process and appropriate procedures are followed. The mentor and supervisor need to work together to assist the intern.

If improvement does not take place or the intern's weaknesses are affecting the learning of the students in the classroom, it may become necessary to eventually consider removing the struggling intern from the assignment. If this occurs, all procedures outlined by the university should take place. Treating this serious decision in the most professional manner ensures that all parties are treated fairly.

CONFERENCING WITH THE STRUGGLING INTERN

Discussing unsatisfactory performance[8] with a struggling intern can be an unpleasant and stressful experience for both the mentor teacher and university supervisor. Using positive confrontation strategies can help make the task easier. Positive confrontation may seem to be a contradiction in terms, but effective supervisors can provide negative feedback to a struggling intern without creating unnecessary conflict.

There are six principles supervisors should follow when conducting conferences with a struggling intern. Conferences with struggling interns usually go more smoothly when the university supervisor participates with the mentor to minimize the stress for the mentor and ensure that all principles are appropriately applied.[9]

Principle 1—Conferences Should Have a Positive Tone

Although negative feedback is involved in conferences with a struggling intern, supervisors need to reflect their concern for the intern and interest in the intern's success. Communicating throughout the conference that an intern's success is the primary goal of the supervisors helps to make the implementation of a supervisor's recommendations for improvement more likely to occur.

Principle 2—Supervisors Need to Lead the Conference and Direct its Outcome

Struggling interns often try to avoid negative feedback by distracting the supervisor or offering excuses. The supervisor needs to deal appropriately with resistance from interns.

Principle 3—The Supervisor Needs to Ensure the Conferences Focus on Key Issues.

Key issues are the problems preventing the intern from being successful and may include lack of skill, inappropriate interactions, or unacceptable attitudes. Again, the intern may try to direct the conference to less important topics, so the supervisor needs to make sure the focus of the conference remains on the important. Remembering to key in on two or three issues will provide the focus needed for a productive conference.

Principle 4—Each Conference Should Include Appropriate and Positive Comments

The intern must realize the mentor and university supervisor are continuing to notice improved and appropriate teaching decisions, behaviors, and attitudes. An intern also needs to be encouraged when progress is made on an area of concern and the efforts an intern is making to improve need to be acknowledged. Improvement does not always occur quickly.

Principle 5—A Plan of Action for Improvement Should be Developed During the Conference

The plan should identify specific areas of concern and specify the expectations for how the intern is going to improve. An appropriate plan might initially include a time frame of a week so that an intern can demonstrate growth in one or two identified areas of improvement. At the end of the predetermined time, the mentor, the university supervisor, and the intern will meet again to determine what progress, if any, has been made and decide the next steps to be taken.

Principle 6—The Conference Needs to Conclude with a Summary of What Has Been Discussed

Supervisors should briefly summarize the concerns, the plan of action, and the time frame. Lopez-Real, Stimpson, and Bunton also identify six characteristics of a conference: identify the problem, understand the situation, provide support, discuss concrete incidents, trust the relationship, and be sensitive to the intern.[10]

If the intern is demonstrating serious problems or improvement is not occurring as expected, it may be useful to develop a contract for the intern that identifies the specific areas of improvement, indicators of the improvements, and a timeline for improvement. Contracts should be aligned with university policies. An example of an improvement contract can be found in Appendix 4.

DEALING WITH RESISTANCE FROM STRUGGLING INTERNS

It is important for the supervisor to remain in control and direct the outcome of the conference. Interns may try to resist[11] the need for improvement by using the following strategies:

- Refusing to acknowledge there is a problem
- Minimizing the seriousness of the problem
- Questioning the objectivity or skill of the supervisor
- Comparing themselves to others who "do it that way"
- Becoming defensive
- Becoming angry
- Blaming other people or circumstances

When an intern refuses to acknowledge that a problem or concern exists, the supervisor should restate the issue and provide appropriate examples. Reminding interns of expectations presented in university policy manuals or evaluation documents may be helpful.

Sometimes, a struggling intern recognizes that a problem exists, but minimizes the seriousness of the problem. The supervisor can counter this resistance by making sure the problem or problems are clearly identified and the reasons for the seriousness are clear. For an intern struggling with classroom management, for example, injury may occur if students are not managed appropriately. If the intern is not treating all students equitably, the students' attitudes toward the subject and school may be affected, and it can negatively impact learning.

When confronted, some interns react by questioning the skill or objectivity[12] of the mentor. It is especially important that the university supervisor be present at these conferences to clarify that such criticism of a mentor is not appropriate. The intern should be refocused to deal with improving her own skills. The conference must remain focused on the concerns and redirect the conference in order to maintain a focus on issues related to the intern's performance. The supervisor can make a note that the intern raised concerns and possibly discuss these concerns at a later meeting.

Some interns respond to negative feedback by comparing themselves to others. Again, it may be helpful to remind an intern of performance expectations. It is seldom useful to compare one's performance with that of another teacher, and it is doubtful that a struggling intern can make such comparisons accurately. Therefore, it is usually best to redirect the conference to focus on the intern's performance.

Unfortunately, some interns respond to negative feedback by becoming defensive, hostile, or angry. It is sometimes effective to respond by describing how the supervisor perceives the intern's attitude and behavior. For example, "You seem to be upset" or "You seem uneasy about our discussion." It is important that the mentor or university supervisor avoid escalating a negative situation by responding with defensiveness, hostility, or anger. If necessary, adjourning the conference until a time when the intern is less emotional may be best. If the intern continues to respond inappropriately in future conferences, it may be helpful to have the department chair or director of field placements participate in the conference.

Some interns blame other people or circumstances for problems that are occurring. It may be appropriate for the supervisor to acknowledge challenges that the intern is facing. It then becomes essential to redirect the conference and insist that the intern understand and assume responsibility for meeting the expectations outlined by the supervisors.

Finally, some interns will give up when the problems being identified seem overwhelming. Supervisors should affirm their belief in the intern's ability to correct the problem. In some situations, this affirming process may be difficult for the supervisor.

When serious problems occur with interns or expected improvement does not occur, an honest and direct approach is required. Problems encountered in an intern's assignment are occasionally so substantive that a discussion about the possibility of removing the intern from the current assignment is necessary. It is the obligation of the university supervisor to ensure that the intern is given the best possible opportunities for success and sometimes an assignment change can accomplish this goal.

The conditions for a new placement must be clearly identified. Expectations for the intern should be clear to all concerned parties before the placement begins. It is also useful to have an agreement or contract signed by the intern at the beginning of the new placement. The agreement should specify the conditions for and specify the requirements of the new placement that must be completed. The agreement may also identify consequences if the new placement is unsuccessful. For example, the intern may be required to wait a year before reapplying to student teach and, at that time, furnish evidence of successful experiences with students as a tutor or paraprofessional.

It is important that university policies for removing unsuccessful interns are publicized and known in advance by interns, mentor teachers, and university supervisors. Orientation meetings with interns should include discussions of the expectations of interns and of the policies and procedures for internship assignments. The university supervisor has a primary responsibility of protecting the due process rights of the intern and ensuring that policies are followed.

From the mentor's point of view, the primary responsibility must be to the students in his classroom. The desire to help an intern having difficulty cannot and should not be a detriment to the learning of students. As mentioned earlier, the mentor usually feels guilty when an intern does not experience success and is often willing to given an intern many second chances. Unfortunately, this can be at the expense of student learning. This must not and cannot be allowed to happen.

Mentors need to remember that it is the intern's primary responsibility to acquire skills necessary to be successful. By agreeing to work with an intern, a mentor provides only an opportunity for a successful, professional experience. Mentors and supervisors cannot guarantee the success of every intern.

FOLLOWING THROUGH WITH THE EVALUATION PROCESS

When plans for the improvement of an intern are made, the mentor teacher and supervisor need to follow up to determine if appropriate progress is occurring. Observational data from visits to the classroom, records of formative conferences, and documentation of the efforts made to assist the intern should be recorded and available if needed. If all of the conferences, feedback, reflective guidance, and specific examples of performance have not improved the intern's teaching, the intern will need to repeat the clinical experience in another setting. It is a good idea for the university to limit the number of repeat attempts that are given to interns.

SUMMARY

It is not unusual for an intern to experience a short term lack of success in clinical experiences. Unskilled and unaware interns can usually improve when remediation and positive confrontation are used appropriately by supervisors. Interns who are unable to make needed improvements or are unwilling to change unproductive behaviors and attitudes provide a more difficult challenge. When working with a struggling intern, the mentor teacher should call on the university supervisor for assistance in conferencing and strategies for the intern. Together, supervisors should formulate appropriate improvement plans, monitor progress, and collect appropriate data to document the efforts made to assist the intern.

APPLYING WHAT YOU HAVE LEARNED

Video 7.1

In this video, https://www.youtube.com/watch?v=rPdFarWNv5U&feature=youtube, you will observe a formative conference between a university supervisor and a struggling intern. As you observe the conference, look for ways that the mentor teacher uses positive tone and clarifying as the conferences with the intern.

Video 7.2

In this video, https://www.youtube.com/watch?v=EER5YVbNqhA, you will observe a conference between a struggling intern and a mentor teacher. As you observe the conference, look for examples of how the mentor teacher is applying the six principles for conferencing with a struggling intern, which were discussed in this chapter.

NOTES

1. Jaruso, J. (1998). "What Cooperating Teacher Case Studies Reveal about Their Phases of Development as Supervisors of Student Teachers." *European Journal of Teacher Education* 21(1), 119–130.
2. https://www.uwosh.edu/coehs/teachered/student-teaching/course/documents/required-readings/the-struggling-student-teacher.pdf
3. http://www.uft.org/files/attachments/tip-toolkit.pdf
4. http://education.byu.edu/ess/mentoring.html
5. http://education.cu-portland.edu/blog/ed-leadership/four-ways-to-coach-a-struggling-teacher/
6. https://www.naeyc.org/files/yc/file/On%20Our%20Minds%20NAEYC.pdf
7. http://www.edutopia.org/discussion/developing-growth-mindset-teachers-and-staff
8. https://hbr.org/2014/06/everything-you-need-to-know-about-negative-feedback/
9. Foyle, H. C., Lyman, L., and Morehead, M. A. (1992). "The Incompetent Student Teacher." New York: Insight Media, videotape.
10. Lopez-Real, F., Stimpson, P., and Bunton, D. (2001). "Supervisory Conferences: An Exploration of Some Difficult Topics." *Journal of Education for Teaching* 27(2), 172.
11. http://blog.bpir.com/human-resources/managing-resistance-to-improvement
12. https://www.linkedin.com/pulse/how-handle-people-who-reject-feedback-kristin-sherry

Chapter Eight

The Excellent Intern

What characteristics identify the excellent future teacher?[1] Excellent interns demonstrate good organizational skills, ambition, enthusiasm, effective use of varied instructional strategies, classroom *with-it-ness*, relating well to others, showing empathy for students, and the ability to learn quickly. Other characteristics of the excellent intern can be found in Table 8.1.

This chapter will discuss strategies for helping high performing interns continue to grow professionally during the clinical experience. This chapter also provides examples of the professional conference, the reflective conference, and the motivational conference, and discusses techniques in conferencing that a mentor teacher can utilize while working with the excellent intern.[2]

Working with excellent interns,[3] although very rewarding, can be as challenging in some ways as working with ineffective ones. Mentor teachers may

Table 8.1. Characteristics of an Excellent Intern

This list is a composite of characteristics of excellent interns identified by mentor teachers participating in training sessions at Emporia State University from 1989 to 2016. They are in alphabetical order, not in order of importance. The mentor teacher may find it useful to highlight those qualities he thinks are of particular importance and share this information with the intern.

Able to build rapport	Accepts feedback	Acts on feedback
Caring	Classroom management skills	Common sense
Conscientious	Cooperative	Creative
Enthusiastic	Flexible	Good planning skills
Honest	Knowledgeable	Motivational
Organized	Personable	Positive attitude
Problem solver	Reliable and responsible	Self-starter
Team player	Wants to be there	

feel frustrated because they do not feel comfortable recommending ideas to high performers. Talvitie, Peltokallio, and Mannisto indicate that interns want more feedback than is typically given by mentors, especially early in the assignment.[4] A common statement often expressed by excellent interns is, "My mentor teacher was great, but she never really offered any specific suggestions or improvement." Since outstanding interns are so talented, mentor teachers often find it difficult to identify areas for improvement.

Most high performing interns want to constantly improve so they are usually very receptive to feedback and are able to apply feedback productively. With increasing student diversity, curriculum standards, and opportunities to use incorporate new instructional strategies and technology,[5] effective teachers will be learning and improving throughout their careers. It is important to remember that even the most capable beginning teacher can continue to improve and grow professionally.

If an intern is doing well with day-to-day classroom instruction and management, a mentor can identify additional areas for reflection and growth. Areas of growth may include using strategies the intern has not tried, such as cooperative learning and integrating Science, Technology, Engineering, and Mathematics (STEM) content into teaching. The mentor may challenge the intern to include more differentiation in his or her teaching such as providing more enrichment activities.

Mentors and supervisors can promote the professional growth of excellent interns by helping them to acquire and enhance these crucial skills:

- Becoming reflective—demonstrated by identifying personal strengths and weaknesses as they relate to teaching. Beginning teachers must start practicing the process for self-evaluation, self-improvement, and reflection so they can become the best possible teacher.
- Expanding the knowledge base—demonstrated by initiative, which leads to self-directed observation, questioning, and outside reading. The outstanding educator is always attempting to increase understanding of the teaching–learning process.
- Creating a vision of their classroom—demonstrated by verbally describing and giving specific examples of the classroom environment, style of instruction, and desired intern interaction. Successful professionals are able to clearly verbalize a vision of their goals and professional environment.

CONFERENCING WITH THE EXCELLENT INTERN

When working with the excellent intern, it is important to encourage the intern to reflect even more effectively on his or her teaching practices and innovations. To encourage professional growth and reflection, the mentor can utilize conferencing techniques mentioned earlier in the book, such as reinforcement, clarification, and brainstorming.

When conferencing with an excellent intern, basic principles to consider are (1) everyone can improve professionally, (2) focus on skills, (3) encourage self-evaluation, (4) recognize professional ethics, and (5) deal directly with the issues at hand. These principles work especially well with excellent interns who are usually eager to improve their teaching.

Successful conferences will help excellent interns in becoming even more professional and reflective while enhancing the professional development of the intern. Although potentially useful for all interns, there are three kinds of conferences that are especially appropriate for the excellent intern: the professional conference, the reflective conference, and the motivational conference.

THE PROFESSIONAL CONFERENCE

Professionalism is demonstrated by maturity,[6] self-direction, positive interpersonal relationships, a positive attitude toward other educators, and a concern for the teaching profession. Early in their careers, outstanding performers sometimes are not tolerant or understanding of others' life situations or professional circumstances.

An excellent intern who has been successful academically and has high expectations for students may not always exhibit appropriate understanding and patience in relationships with students or colleagues. For example, interns may not be sympathetic to the life circumstances and developmental levels of students in the classroom. The intern may show impatience with the student who does not put forth enough effort. Interns who are high achievers may not relate effectively to those students who cannot meet expectations. Most excellent interns are responsive to feedback, so a discussion about students who need more patience and empathy will most likely modify the intern's behavior and attitudes.

Early in some professionals' careers, rushing to judgment about other educators without understanding or knowing background information can occur. As with interns who are impatient or lack empathy with lower performing students, the mentor's feedback can help the intern to reflect on his or her attitudes and behavior and make appropriate professional changes.

The mentor can design a professional conference to promote positive changes when impatience, lack of empathy, and intolerance of students or other educators are observed by the mentor. The mentor should decide which approach is best suited to the intern and to the circumstances when deciding how to begin the conference. For example, should the conference begin with a question, statement, or a description of the situation?

During the conference, the mentor will help the intern to identify the behaviors and attitudes that need to be changed. Together, the mentor and intern will determine ways in which the intern can deal directly with the situation and become more understanding and effective. The mentor may want to share personal experiences that relate to the situation when appropriate.

It may be helpful to have the intern write a brief description of her perception about the student(s) or other professionals.[7]

As with any effective conference, the mentor needs to identify suggestions or strategies that would assist the intern in identifying and changing behavior prior to the conference. The mentor should decide on only one or two specific events or behaviors to discuss during the conference. As the mentor notices the desired improvement taking place, the mentor will provide positive feedback to encourage the intern to continue to improve.

THE REFLECTIVE CONFERENCE

The reflective conference deals with an intern who is always charging ahead and cannot wait for the next *new* opportunity. Becoming reflective is demonstrated by identifying personal strengths and weaknesses as they relate to teaching. Beginning teachers must practice the process of self-evaluation and self-improvement. The reflective conference is useful when meeting with this *thoroughbred* intern. This intern usually cannot wait for the next opportunity to teach and try new teaching strategies. Their minds work quickly, and they exude tremendous energy and confidence. However, sometimes an outstanding beginning professional tries too many different and innovative approaches without refining their instruction and doing the necessary professional reflection for these approaches to be most effective. The intern may become overwhelmed[8] and less productive when trying too many new ideas and approaches.

Without dampening the intern's enthusiasm, the mentor should assist in modifying these practices and emphasize ongoing reflection and instructional refinement to help the intern avoid unnecessary stress and burnout.

A reflective conference with an excellent intern can help the intern focus on how they can be most productive. As with any intern, it may be helpful to provide the excellent intern with specific examples for improving instruction. The mentor can provide appropriate reinforcement for strategies which the intern is using effectively.

During the reflective conference, the mentor can provide specific examples of how she approaches improving, modifying, and implementing instruction.

For example, this might include methods in which accreditation standards and state assessment practices are incorporated into daily classroom lessons.[9]

The most important part of the reflection conference is helping the intern to reflect upon his or her experiences and be an active participant in identifying and implementing needed changes.[10] The mentor may need to provide examples of how the intern is becoming less effective or overwhelmed to encourage productive reflection. Sharing personal approaches to conserving energy and eliciting reflection about teaching experiences are important supervisory responsibilities. As the intern learns to manage his or her passion for teaching more effectively, stress can be reduced and productivity, increased.[11]

THE MOTIVATIONAL CONFERENCE

The motivational conference is effective for the excellent intern who may be hesitant to try new ideas and strategies. Interns who may be teaching effectively and are perceived as excellent by others, is uneasy about exploring new strategies, possibly due to the fear of failing. Professional growth requires the intern to be open to trying new strategies and the motivational conference can help to guide an intern toward reaching her full potential.[12]

When encouraging interns to try new strategies and approaches, it is useful to reinforce the things that the intern is doing effectively. The intern needs to understand that he or she has the ability to be successful with new approaches because of past successes.

The intern must be challenged to reach beyond his or her comfort zone. During the motivational conference, the mentor and intern can brainstorm one or two strategies to try that encourage risk taking. Since excellent interns are usually focused on the success of the students, it is helpful to identify the probable benefits for students if new strategies are implemented.

When the intern tries a new strategy, reinforcement from the mentor will encourage the intern to continue to try new strategies. Some interns require a great deal of encouragement to become "responsible risk takers" who are comfortable trying new approaches and strategies.

ADDITIONAL STRATEGIES FOR WORKING WITH EXCELLENT INTERNS

When working with excellent interns, clarification and brainstorming are especially appropriate conferencing strategies. Clarification questions can help the excellent intern reflect on his or her teaching and articulate the reasons for teaching decisions. Appropriate use of clarification can also help the excellent intern identify alternative strategies and approaches to try in future lessons. Brainstorming can encourage the intern to come up with creative ways to meet the needs of the students in the classroom.

All interns benefit from opportunities to become more reflective about their teaching. A very effective way for interns to reflect is to make a video while they are teaching. The excellent intern may be encouraged to reflect on different aspects of his or her performance when observing videos of their teaching.

Some excellent interns may be too critical of themselves and may focus on areas that need improvement more than areas in which they are doing well. Mentors need to encourage interns who are unduly critical of themselves to recognize their strengths and use those strengths to continue to grow and develop professionally. Clarification questions can help the intern to identify these strengths.

The ultimate goal when working with an excellent intern is to develop a peer relationship—one that indicates to both parties that they view each other as equals in the profession. Justen and McJunkin discuss the nondirective approach to supervision and affirm the importance of trust and mutual respect. The nondirective approach in supervising will allow the intern the necessary reflection time to develop this peer relationship.[13]

SUMMARY

Excellent interns bring many strengths into the clinical assignment: they learn quickly, are well organized, are self-starting, demonstrate enthusiasm, vary instructional strategies, have classroom *with-it-ness*, relate well with others, and show empathy for their students. These qualities can be positive assets in working with students and colleagues.

Mentor teachers should not be intimidated by the abilities of outstanding interns. Mentors have skills, qualities, and expertise that can assist the excellent intern's professional growth as a reflective, knowledgeable, and empathetic practitioner. The university supervisor can be helpful if concerns do develop.

Because they are high performers, excellent interns may lack patience and tolerance for less capable students and colleagues. Professional conferences led by the mentor can help the intern to the interpersonal qualities needed to be truly successful.

The enthusiasm of the excellent intern may cause him or her to take on too many things without appropriate balance and reflection. Interns can become overwhelmed when this occurs. The reflective conference provides an opportunity to help the intern focus on key issues and prioritize.

Some excellent interns may avoid trying new strategies that are outside of their comfort zone. Mentors can use motivational conferences to encourage interns to work harder to reach their potential as teachers.

Excellent interns grow professionally when they are challenged by opportunities to clarify and brainstorm during conferences and to critique their performance through videotaping. Mentors and supervisors can be invaluable resources to the intern who needs help in identifying professional strengths as well as areas for improvement.

The influence of the mentor and intern on the growth and development of the excellent intern, or any intern they may work with, is influenced by the quality of the relationship that develops between supervisor and intern. With excellent interns, trust and mutual respect is especially important. Nondirective supervision may be an effective strategy in working with excellent interns.

APPLYING WHAT YOU HAVE LEARNED

Video 8.1

In Video 8.1, https://www.youtube.com/watch?v=itK3bbFr1ck, you will observe a conference between a supervisor and an excellent intern who is working in a kindergarten classroom. As you observe the conference, look for ways in which the intern demonstrates that she is an excellent intern.

Video 8.2

In Video 8.2, https://www.youtube.com/watch?v=Z0cb9Gp-GFE, you will observe a portion of a conference between a supervisor and an intern assigned to a fourth grade classroom. As you observe the conference, look for strategies that the supervisor uses to encourage the intern to reflect on her teaching during the conference.

NOTES

1. https://teachingcommons.stanford.edu/resources/teaching/planning-your-approach/characteristics-effective-teachers

2. Foyle, H., Lyman, L., and Morehead, M. (1992). "The Excellent Student Teacher." New York: Insight Media, videotape.

3. https://pridestaff.com/sites/default/files/resources/PS-Overachievers_2013_FINAL.pdf

4. Talvitie, U., Peltokallio, L., and Mannisto, P. (2000). "Student Teachers' Views about Their Relationships with University Supervisors, Cooperating Teachers, and Peer Student Teachers." *Scandinavian Journal of Educational Research* 44(1), 83.

5. http://www.edutopia.org/discussion/15-characteristics-21st-century-teacher

6. http://www.coachingpositiveperformance.com/12-signs-of-emotional-maturity/

7. Silva, D. Y. (2000). "Triad Journaling as a Tool for Reconceptualizing Supervision in the Professional Development School." Proceedings from American Educational Research Association, New Orleans, 1–17.

8. http://thinksimplenow.com/productivity/overwhelmed/?utm_source=feedburner&utm_medium=feed&utm_campaign=Feed:+ThinkSimple+(Think+Simple+Now)

9. Giebelhaus, C. and Bowman, C. (2000). "Teaching Mentors: Is It Worth the Effort?" Proceedings from Association of Teacher Educators, Orlando, Florida, 1–24.

10. Cruickshank, D. (1987). *Reflective Teaching: The Preparation of Students of Teaching.* Reston, Virginia: Association of Teacher Educators.

11. http://www.forbes.com/sites/travisbradberry/2014/02/06/how-successful-people-stay-calm/#1d40bb6e9c8c

12. https://hbr.org/2011/06/managing-yourself-the-paradox-of-excellence

13. Justen III, J. and McJunkin, M. (1999). "Supervisor Beliefs of Cooperating Teachers." *Teacher Educator* 34(3), 179.

Chapter Nine

The Principal's Role

As the primary instructional leader[1] of the school, the principal should take an active role in the Professional Development School partnership and in working with interns. It is difficult for many principals to find the necessary time to play this active role because of the many other factors that compete for their time. In order to ensure that interns are a positive addition to the school, however, the principal needs to be involved in decisions involving resources, selection, supervision, and evaluation of interns in his or her building. With the evolution of professional development schools (PDS) the principal's role is changing dramatically because of the need to collaborate in a more formal manner with teacher education programs.

HOW THE PRINCIPAL SUPPORTS MENTOR TEACHERS AND INTERNS

Principals have numerous responsibilities[2] that demand on their time. The principal's active involvement in providing leadership and support, supporting effective curriculum and instructional strategies, managing resources, and helping to facilitate the PDS partnership can require a commitment of time and energy.

The principal's leadership and support[3] is essential to the success of a PDS partnership. When a climate for collaboration[4] between teachers and administrators has been established, collaboration with teacher education programs is a natural extension of these productive relationships. Teachers and principals who collaborate effectively together can better nurture the professional association that needs to be developed between the school and the teacher education program. In addition, the principal can also demonstrate his or her commitment to collaboration by attending meetings involving the PDS, including training sessions. This involvement is a very profound statement on the part of the principal because of the time commitment required.

The principal's knowledge of best practices in teaching and his or her ability to focus the energy and resources of teachers on improving student achievement defines an instructional leader.[5] Collaboration between the principal, mentor teachers, and university faculty as part of a PDS program will enhance the schools' access to the latest strategies for improving student achievement, including curriculum and instructional strategies. The principal's leadership helps to create a climate that allows the school to access the knowledge available through the partnership with the teacher education program.

One of the benefits from the PDS partnership is the opportunity for mentor teachers and teacher education faculty to study the impact of the new strategies and programs on students. As new ideas emerge, the principal provides encouragement for innovation and helps to direct the necessary resources to make innovation successful.

Effective principals are effective in managing the financial and human resources of the school. Successful partnerships with teacher education programs can enhance resources available to the school by bringing interns who provide extra support for students and mentor teachers into the classroom. Ongoing planning with teachers and university staff can also assist the school in providing additional services to students using other university resources. For example, Hermosa Heights Elementary School, which has been a PDS site for over ten years with New Mexico State University, is now provided with services for students that include counseling interns and administrative interns. These additional resources provide assistance to students, teachers, and families that would not be available without the partnership.

As the PDS partnership matures, the principal can work with the university to involve additional program support in terms of science experts,[6] math experts, and social work specialists if the university has such programs. Additionally, university students and faculty can attend and participate in collaborative professional development programs that broaden the expertise of these individuals and therefore become resources for the students in the school.

Principals can also work with teachers and university personnel to enhance the financial resources available to the school because foundations, state and national agencies often look for collaborative efforts to support. Professional development schools have an advantage when applying for grants[7] because of the collaboration. University faculty are often expected to write for grants and have access to resources that can assist them in preparing the grant proposals. Also community agencies and companies are much more likely to offer financial support when the K–12 arena collaborates with teacher education.

Effective principals have the skills and commitment to have an important impact on the implementation of PDS program. According to Gutierrez, productive partnerships should result in an energized and innovative environment.[8] In such an environment, teachers, interns, and university faculty would be involved in a variety of instructional activities, creating a community that is reflective, innovative, creative, and collaborative. In a successful PDS, an observer might not be able to tell who was the intern, the master teacher, or university faculty member.

Productive partnerships can only be sustained through extensive collaboration and mutual respect.[9] The principal helps to facilitate collaboration and respect and enhance them by creating effective teams and by nurturing a reflective approach to problem solving that honors all views and opinions.

BENEFITS OF INTERNS

Principals recognize that interns have many potential benefits[10] for a school. Effective interns can be valuable additions to inclusive classrooms with diverse students whose varying needs require more time and energy. In effect, a competent intern helps to lower the pupil–teacher ratio in a given classroom. Interns also bring enthusiasm and idealism into the school setting. The fresh perspective of the intern can be refreshing to both principals and teachers.

Interns have the potential to bring new and updated strategies for working with students into the school. For example, interns may be well prepared to work with second language learners. They may be able to assist the mentor teacher in using different strategies to meet the needs of students in the diverse classrooms of today. For example, interns may be well prepared to work with second language learners due to the growth of multicultural classes and second language learner classes in teacher education programs. Interns often bring new strategies for using technology[11] into the classroom as well.

Having an intern in the classroom usually encourages the mentor to be more conscious of teaching decisions being made. An intern's questions may cause the mentor to be more reflective[12] about why certain strategies are being used and how those strategies impact student learning and the classroom environment.

With interns come university supervisors who are usually willing to provide assistance to teachers in the school who are trying new strategies or who are able to identify other faculty members with particular expertise. University professors may be willing to practice and refine their own teaching skills by working in classrooms themselves.[13]

ALLOCATING RESOURCES

The resources required to support interns can become somewhat of a challenge, especially with declining school budgets.[14] For example, many school districts require background checks for interns and a decision needs to be made as to whether interns, most of whom face financial challenges, will pay the cost of a background check that the district requires.

Interns use supplies, which may strain financial resources even further. For example, interns may need to copy evaluation documents using school resources. A generous mentor teacher may encourage the intern to duplicate his or her files for their own use. Interns may also find resources in the school media center that they want to duplicate. Principals need to determine whether the cost of these copies is provided as a benefit to the intern because of what he or she is contributing to the school, or if the intern should be expected to pay for copies made for his or her later professional use.

If interns are using consumable supplies such as lamination film, computer supplies, construction paper, file folders, and the like to prepare materials for use in the clinical experience, few principals would reasonably expect the intern to pay for these supplies or to leave the completed instructional materials at the school when the intern leaves. The cost of such materials, however, may add up if too many interns come to the school. Principals need to define policies regarding the use of supplies by interns and make these policies clear to the interns.

The addition of extra people to a school takes resources that are often in short supply. For example, interns utilize parking spaces that may be limited. School staff may find the staff bathrooms and faculty lounge more crowded when interns are part of the school. The telephone or copy machine may be unavailable because of intern use. Because the resources at most schools are limited, principals need to determine how many interns are appropriate for a given building each semester and work with mentor teachers to create appropriate guidelines for the responsible use of school resources by interns.

SELECTION OF MENTOR TEACHERS

One of the principal's most important responsibilities is identifying mentor teachers who are well qualified for the challenges of working with future teachers. Many universities ask for the input of the principal in determining which teachers are effective,[15] thus making them good candidates for mentor teachers. Teachers who are effective in the classroom are not automatically good candidates for mentor teachers as some do not work as effectively with adults as they do with students. Principals also need to determine which teachers actually want to work with interns as well which teachers are qualified to do so.

In general, mentor teachers should have a minimum of three years of experience. The potential mentor should be knowledgeable about the content taught and about current strategies for teaching. Good classroom management skills and the ability to relate positively with students is a must for a mentor teacher. It is essential that mentor teachers consistently model excellent communication and interpersonal skills in working with colleagues, administrators, and family members.

Because of the potential benefits of having interns in the school, principals will occasionally agree to an intern placement without checking with the potential mentor teacher. The mentor teacher should always be able to choose whether or not they wish to work with an intern in a given semester. The mentor should always have the opportunity for a personal interview with a potential intern, if desired, before agreeing to accept the placement.

Principals may have requests for interns from teachers who the principal feels are not well suited to be a mentor teacher. For example, a potential mentor who has been teaching for several years might indicate to an intern that the extensive lesson plans and reflection expected by the university are not necessary. These comments may undermine the expectations of the university and conflict with the expectations outlined to the intern. When mentors do not support the university program, it may set the intern up for limited success or failure and creates potential conflict between the university and mentor teacher.

Another example is the mentor teacher who does not give feedback and is unable or unwilling to offer corrective guidance when necessary. This teacher may be terrific with students but may not communicate as effectively with adults. This can create a climate of distrust and may lead to an intern receiving an evaluation he or she did not expect. These examples indicate the importance of the principal being aware of the strengths and weakness of teachers in his or her school when making recommendations for potential mentor teachers.

Infrequently, principals may recommend a placement for a strong intern to work with a teacher who is experiencing problems in the classroom because of weak teaching, poor classroom management, health issues, or other factors. It is absolutely inappropriate to place an intern, no matter how skilled, in a setting where they do not have opportunities to work with a strong, positive mentor who models effective teaching strategies and who can provide the feedback necessary for an intern to grow professionally.

Professional Development Schools programs tend to alleviate problems with ineffective mentor teachers because of the extensive communication that exists between schools and teacher education programs. It should be agreed that both the principal and the university must agree when a placement is made. For example, a principal may want a mentor teacher to have an intern in his or her classroom, but the university may disagree based on feedback from university supervisors and previous interns. The decision on the part of the university not to place interns with a particular mentor teacher should be made with the utmost care and should be supported by the principal. Although these decisions put stress on relationships, they are necessary to ensure that interns have the most productive clinical experiences possible.

MAKING INTERNS A PART OF THE SCHOOL

The principal can help interns by meeting with mentor teachers before interns arrive to make sure mentor teachers are aware of district and building policies that may affect their interns and to discuss issues that may impact interns. Some of the topics to be clarified include the following:

- When is it appropriate to leave the intern alone with students?
- When can the intern assume playground duty, bus duty, or other duty assignments?
- What is the policy for interns on reporting suspected child abuse?
- What kinds of lesson plans are to be turned as interns assume teaching responsibilities?
- How are interns to be involved in staff meetings and inservices?
- How are interns to be involved in staff functions?
- If a social fee is collected from staff, will interns to pay all or part of this fee?
- How are interns to be involved in school improvement plans for the school?
- What is the expected dress for interns?

In addition to working with mentors to identify policies and guidelines for interns, the principal can help to assure that every intern feels welcome in the school. The arrival of interns should be announced in the school bulletin. Interns should be introduced to the staff at a faculty meeting.

Parents and guardians also need to be informed when an intern will be working in their student's classroom. A note in the school newsletter can introduce interns to parents and guardians and provide some background information. The principal will also want to encourage the mentor teacher to send a note to parents and guardians letting them know about the intern's background and what his or her responsibilities will be in the classroom. Mentors may choose to have the intern write the note to parents and guardians. Mentors need to carefully proofread and edit any communication from an intern to family members and the principal may also want to read the note before it is sent home.

Principals will want to have an orientation meeting with the interns assigned to the building early each semester. During this meeting, the principal will want to share basic information about the school and appropriate district and building policies. The principal should also share his or her expectations for interns at the school. Some of the information for this meeting may be found in Appendix 2.

SUPERVISION OF INTERNS

Although the mentor teacher shares the primary responsibility for supervision of the intern with the university supervisor, the principal will want to look over conference notes, assessment forms, and lesson plans to determine how well interns are doing. Positive reinforcement, in person or in a note, lets the intern know that the principal is interested in the progress that the intern is making.

If time permits, the principal should plan a formal classroom observation for each intern at least once during the intern's assignment. As an experienced supervisor, the principal can provide valuable feedback to the intern about his or her strengths and weaknesses in the classroom.

Many principals use walk through supervision[16] visits to keep up on what is going on in classrooms and provide feedback to teachers about their effectiveness. When interns are present in the classroom, these visits provide an opportunity to provide feedback to interns on a regular basis. Some principals are willing to take the time to schedule practice interviews[17] with interns. This is a real benefit to intern who are usually nervous about the interview process and unsure about how to prepare. By providing feedback about strong and weak points of a practice interview, the principal provides valuable professional assistance to the future teacher.

SUMMARY

The principal of the school where interns are working has several responsibilities for their success. As the instructional leader of the school, the principal is responsible for establishing a collaborative climate that nurtures effective instruction for diverse students. The principal needs to make sure that resources at the school are adequate for the number of interns placed at the school and that appropriate procedures are in place for interns' use of resources.

The principal should assure that mentor teachers are willing and qualified to work with an intern and that appropriate supervision of interns is taking place. Working with mentor teachers, the principal assures that expectations for interns are clear and that interns feel welcome in the school. Principals become an active participant in the intern's professional development by checking the progress of the intern by monitoring conference notes and evaluation forms from mentor teachers and assessing lessons plans submitted by interns. Feedback that results from scheduled observations or walk through supervision visits can be an important supplement to the feedback provided to interns by mentors and university supervisors. Practice conferences with interns are another way that principals can assist future teachers.

APPLYING WHAT YOU HAVE LEARNED

Video 9.1

In video 9.1, https://youtu.be/pIlH-ZCU5WM, a veteran PDS principal discusses benefits of the PDS program. What are some of the benefits that the principal identifies for the schools he has served as a PDS principal?

NOTES

1. http://www.naesp.org/sites/default/files/LeadershipMatters.pdf
2. http://www.edweek.org/ew/articles/2014/03/26/26principals_ep.h33.html
3. https://www.naesp.org/resources/1/Principal/2008/M-Jp52.pdf
4. http://www.edutopia.org/blog/when-teachers-and-administrators-collaborate-anne-obrien
5. http://inclusiveschools.org/the-principals-responsibilities-in-supporting-quality-instruction/
6. https://www.emporia.edu/news/03/07/2016/stem-grant-to-benefit-fredonia-altoona-neodesha-schools/
7. http://www.schoolfundingcenter.info/
8. Gutierrez, C., Field, S., Basile, C., and Simmons, J. (2007). "Principals as knowledge managers: Helping principals of professional development schools intentionally utilize the resources of the partnership." *School-University Partnerships* 1(2), 42–54.
9. http://inquiry.galileo.org/ch6/instructional-leadership/creating-a-culture-of-creativity-risk-taking-and-innovation/
10. http://www.usnews.com/opinion/knowledge-bank/articles/2016-03-23/better-clinical-teaching-preparation-benefits-school-districts-and-students
11. https://www.emporia.edu/teach/hcl/

12. https://dashthebook.wordpress.com/2015/03/28/student-teacher-the-best-of-both-worlds/

13. Lyman, L. (2000, February). "A Professor Returns to the Classroom in a Professional Development School." ERIC Resources in Education. Paper presented at the national conference of the Kansas University Professional Development Schools Alliance, Kansas City, Missouri.

14. http://www.cbpp.org/research/state-budget-and-tax/most-states-have-cut-school-funding-and-some-continue-cutting

15. http://educationnext.org/files/ednext20062_58.pdf

16. https://www.naesp.org/resources/2/Principal/2009/M-A_p30.pdf

17. http://www.educationworld.com/a_admin/admin/admin071.shtml

Chapter Ten

Training for Mentor Teachers and University Supervisors

Effective mentor teachers and university supervisors are essential to the professional growth and development of interns during their clinical experiences. All mentor teachers and university supervisors should successfully complete required training.

PURPOSES OF MENTOR AND SUPERVISOR TRAINING

Training helps beginning and experienced mentor teachers and university supervisors to be successful in working with future teachers. All mentors and supervisors should participate in beginning training before working with an intern. As the mentor and supervisor gain experience in working with interns, additional training can enhance skills, provide opportunities to learn specialized skills, and provide opportunities for recalibrating the skills of the mentor. Meetings with mentors and supervisors can provide opportunities for informal training.

Before working with an intern, mentors and supervisors should successfully complete training to learn about the goals and framework of the teacher education program. This training should include goals to learn about the assessments used in the program and the responsibility the mentor and supervisor have for completing those assessments, to learn about the role of the mentor teacher, and to learn supervision skills. Important concepts for beginning training are listed in Table 10.1.

Opportunities to apply the information provided in the training and to practice supervision skills is essential. During the training, it is important for beginning mentors and supervisors to have frequent chances to interact with the trainers and other participants and to ask questions. In previous chapters

Table 10.1. Content for Beginning Mentor Teacher Training

Goals and Conceptual Framework of the Teacher Education Program
Roles of the Mentor Teacher and University Supervisor
Curriculum and Admission Requirements for Interns
Expectations for Interns
Formative and Summative Assessments
Supervision Skills for Mentors and Supervisors
Practice and Application

---

of this book, communication and supervision skills which mentors and supervisors need to be successful have been identified. Training in these skills with opportunities to practice the skills is another crucial part of beginning mentor and supervisor training. Content from this book, including video segments, can be helpful in organizing a beginning training program[1] which is compatible with the goals of the teacher training program.

University supervisors are the liaison between interns, mentors, and the university. It is helpful for university supervisors to participate in the same beginning training as mentor teachers but supervisors need additional training to assure that they are familiar with the policies and procedures of the teacher education program and that they demonstrate the interpersonal skills needed to be effective. Because university supervisors play a crucial role in working with struggling interns, the additional training they receive should also address the appropriate remediation efforts that need to take place, the university policies which must be followed, and due process that needs to be accorded to a struggling intern.

After beginning training is completed, additional training can provide mentors and supervisors with opportunities to enhance their skills in working with interns. Because conferencing skills[2] are crucial for effectiveness, advanced training provides additional instruction and practice in effective communication and conferencing with interns. Because struggling interns are often a concern of mentors and supervisors, specific strategies for working with interns who are struggling could be a productive focus of advanced training sessions. Through communication with mentors and supervisors and looking at feedback from interns who have completed the program, other areas for advanced training can be identified.

Training that helps mentors and supervisors acquire specialized skills for working with interns can also be useful. Because interns who have been unsuccessful in previous clinical placements can provide particular challenges for mentors and supervisors, providing specialized training in working with repeating interns is a possibility. Experienced mentors who have been successful in working with a number of interns would be invited to participate in the specialized training and would receive additional compensation for working with a repeating intern.

In order to assure that there is inter-rater reliability[3] among the mentors and supervisors using the formative and summative assessments in the program, it is helpful to provide an opportunity for recalibration. Recalibration could provide an opportunity for mentors and supervisors to rate a videotaped lesson using the assessments required by the program. After the evaluation is completed, mentors and supervisors can discuss the results and their rationale for the ratings they made. Those in charge of the program can compare the ratings to determine accuracy and reliability.

At the PDS site, coordinators frequently meet with mentor teachers. These meetings provide opportunities for informal training sessions as well as updates about the program. It is a good idea for university supervisors to meet as well for informal training and updates. These informal training sessions can address specific questions of the mentors at a particular PDS site or concerns of university supervisors who work with interns.

COMPONENTS OF EFFECTIVE TRAINING

In order to maximize the efforts of those who conduct mentor and supervisor training and those who participate in the training, effective planning and organization[4] is crucial. Clearly articulated objectives for training which are aligned with the goals of the teacher training program are necessary to make appropriate use of available time. Because most mentors and supervisors will have high expectations for training, trainers[5] need to be familiar with the content to be presented and able to model effective instructional strategies during the training.

Effective training programs are geared toward the needs of adult learners.[6] For example, it is important that training sessions take place in locations where seating and tables are designed for adults. Training should take place in a room with good acoustics, where participants can clearly see any materials displayed on screens, and where interaction with other participants is facilitated.

A variety of appropriate instructional strategies should be modeled in training programs so that the learning styles of the participants are accommodated. Opportunities for listening, viewing, interacting, and applying content should be provided during training sessions.

Video segments, such as those in this book, can provide opportunities for mentors and supervisors to apply concepts and skills they are learning.

Group building activities[7] can help mentors and supervisors get to know each other and help to make training sessions more interactive and enjoyable.

Table 10.2. Sample People Search Activity for Mentor and Supervisor Training

Find someone who

is a former (name of university) PDS intern	has been teaching for 10 years or more	has been teaching for less than 5 years
has another family member who is a teacher	has supervised a student teacher before	has good classroom management
has two or more children	has one or more grandchildren	owns two or more dogs
has travelled outside the United States	likes to try new kinds of technology	likes to work out

Ideally, all of the participants in a training session would have the opportunity to work together in at least one activity. For example, a people search activity can encourage interaction and movement (Table 10.2).

Additional examples of group building activities can be found in the videos which follow this chapter.

Mentors and supervisors bring many experiences and ideas when they come to training. Participants in training sessions benefits from opportunities to share real life examples of effective strategies they use for communication, interaction with others, instruction, and classroom management.

Real life examples can also be included in training by using videos of intern lessons and conferences between interns and supervisors. There are a number of examples in this book of such videos. It may be productive for training programs to include videos that include students, mentors, and supervisors from their own programs.

Having opportunities to apply what is being learned is another important component of effective mentor and supervisor training. For example, participants can design and role play an instructional conference after observing an intern's lesson. In addition to providing an opportunity to apply skills from the training, participants get feedback on how well they are learning the skills.

Trainers need to observe mentors and supervisors during activities where skills are practiced and applied in order to determine what to do next in the training process. Mentors and supervisors who may need additional practice and coaching before they are ready to work with interns may be identified if efforts to apply skills are not successful.

Evaluation is another important component of the training process. At the conclusion of the training, participants can provide crucial feedback to help improve the quality of future training sessions. For example, participants may be able to recommend changes in the format of the training which could

Table 10.3 Sample Evaluation Form for Mentor and Supervisor Training

_____ University
Mentor Teacher and University Supervisor Training
Participant's Evaluation
(date of training)

Please circle the appropriate response for each statement below and include any comments you feel would be helpful.

5 = Strongly agree   4 = Agree   3 = Neutral   2 = Disagree   1 = Strongly disagree

1. This training helped me to better understand the university's expectations for PDS mentor teachers.	1	2	3	4	5
2. The training helped me enhance my skills as a mentor teacher.	1	2	3	4	5
3. The format of the training facilitated my learning.	1	2	3	4	5
4. The materials used in the training were helpful	1	2	3	4	5
5. I would recommend this training to others who are interested in working with PDS interns.	1	2	3	4	5

Comments

_____
Signature (optional)

increase its effectiveness. Content which the participants would like to see added to the training may be identified. Evaluation also helps to identify what is effective about the training so that these components can be included in future training. An example of an evaluation form can be found in Table 10.3.

INCENTIVES FOR TRAINING

Prospective mentor teachers and university supervisors have many demands on their time. To encourage participation in training and to recognize the efforts made by mentors and supervisors to add training activities to already busy schedules, incentives for participation may be provided. Possible incentives may include payment, opportunity for university credit, and points from district Professional Development Councils.

Payment of an honorarium or stipend for participating in mentor and supervisor training recognizes that the time and effort of the mentor and supervisor are valuable. Even a small stipend can be a way to let mentors and supervisors know that their time and expertise are appreciated. Providing funding for travel appeals to many university supervisors.

Providing university credit for participation in training sessions may be appealing to teachers who are seeking recertification or looking for elective credits for an advanced degree. Some universities are permitted by their governing boards to give tuition-free credit for activities like mentor and supervisor training. If allowed by university rules and policies, this option may be less costly than actually paying mentors and supervisors.

Because Professional Development Schools are partnerships with local education agencies, it may be possible for the school district to offer Professional Development Council points for participating in mentor teacher training activities. The district may allow the university personnel who facilitate the training to provide the required verification of participation in the activity.

University supervisors may benefit from being able to include training activities as part of their goals for achieving tenure and promotion or for merit pay. The administrators of the academic department or unit to which the supervisor is attached can work with training facilitators to document the participation of the supervisor and assist in providing ways to evaluate the growth of the supervisor after participating in the training activities.

One of the best incentives for participating in mentor teacher and university supervisor training is the professional satisfaction of experiencing motivating and challenging training activities which promote professional interaction and fuel professional growth. It is important that those who participate in training have a positive experience so the recommendations they pass on to colleagues encourage them to participate future training sessions.

USING THE RESOURCES IN THIS BOOK TO GET STARTED OR ENHANCE MENTOR AND SUPERVISOR TRAINING

When creating or evaluating beginning training programs, it is suggested that teacher education faculty form a committee of teachers who have supervised the university's future teachers, of graduates of the teacher training program, and other stakeholders such as administrators and teachers from the PDS school sites, faculty who supervise interns, and representatives from community college partnerships. The members of the committee will be responsible for identifying the goals and the content of the training. Table 10.1 can provide suggestions for the content of a beginning program.

The chapters in this book can help trainers organize the content for a beginning training program. It may be useful to provide copies of the book to training participants to use during the training and as a resource for mentors and supervisors to use after training has been completed.

The video segments in this book can be used as part of a training program to model concepts and strategies for mentors and supervisors. When using the videos, it is important to promote discussion and interaction among training participants and the Applying What You Have Learned material in each chapter can offer ideas for trainers to use in those discussions. Hopefully, the material in this chapter will provide guidelines and suggestions to help structure a successful mentor and supervisor training program.

SUMMARY

In order for mentor teachers and university supervisors to be successful in their roles, it is incumbent on the teacher education program to provide appropriate training. Beginning training should be required of all mentors and supervisors. The structure of the teacher education program, including goals, conceptual framework, requirements, and expectations, should be an important part of the content of beginning training. Mentors and supervisors should also have opportunities during beginning training to learn and enhance their communication and supervision skills, with opportunities to practice the skills in real life situations.

Advanced training can be provided to focus on specific issues which arise from mentor and supervisor experiences or from evaluations from interns. Struggling interns are a common concern of mentors and supervisors, and advanced training can focus on this issue. Specialized training can provide opportunities for experienced mentors who have been successful in working with interns to expand their skills and take on additional roles as mentors. Recalibration is necessary periodically to provide quality control for mentors and supervisors.

Components of effective training help to assure a productive experience for mentors and supervisors who participate in the training. Effective planning and organization and knowledgeable trainers are essential to productive training experiences. Consideration of adult learners' needs and varying the instructional strategies used are also important. Successful training sessions include opportunities for interaction among participants which may be encouraged by group building activities. Opportunities to practice skills during training sessions promotes engagement and allows the trainers to evaluate the effectiveness of the training and identify problems or concerns with participants.

Incentives can encourage participation and engagement in training. Stipends, university credit, PDC points, and travel funding are some possibilities for incentives.

Mentor and supervisor training programs can be designed which make use of this book. Content from the chapters and video segments which accompany the chapters can provide some of the content for the training sessions and serve as a reference for participants and trainers.

APPLYING WHAT YOU HAVE LEARNED

Video 10.1

In this video, https://www.youtube.com/watch?v=feE_jCiuh0w, you will observe an activity with mentor teachers who are participating in a training session. As you watch the activity, identify the strategies that the facilitator is using to actively involve the interns as they discuss struggling interns.

Video 10.2

In this video, https://youtu.be/7DVDiljEs8c, you will observe an activity with mentor teachers who are participating in a training session that involves the use of technology. As you watch the activity, look for ways in which the technology activity worked well and identify any drawbacks from using technology in this training activity.

Video 10.3

In this video, https://www.youtube.com/watch?v=x2ccyngdVlo, you will observe an activity with mentor teachers who are participating in a training session. As you watch the activity, identify how the activity promotes critical thinking and active involvement with the participants.

NOTES

1. http://www.emporia.edu/teach/elecse/elemed/pds-training.html
2. http://assist.educ.msu.edu/ASSIST/school/together/seciiplc/seciicment/conferenceskills.html
3. http://www.socialresearchmethods.net/kb/reltypes.php
4. http://www.eiu.edu/ihec/EffectiveTraingConsensusIHEC.pdf
5. https://phasetwolearning.wordpress.com/tag/training-facilitator-best-practices/
6. http://www.fastfamilysupport.org/fasttraining/Other/teachingadults-what trainersneedtoknow.pdf
7. https://docs.google.com/viewer?a=v&pid=sites&srcid=ZGVmYXVsdGRvbW Fpbnxjb3JreXNjb21tdW5pdGllc3xneDo3YzNkZjE4YTY4Nzk3YWUz

Appendix 1

Feedback for Applying What You Have Learned Videos

VIDEO 1.1

Benefits of PDS partnerships discussed in the video included

- model is borrowed from hospital model, future teachers are immersed in the school setting;
- mentor teachers provide feedback, modeling, and inspiration to PDS interns;
- success of the program is supported by evidence and feedback from school partners;
- P–12 students benefit from having interns in the classroom;
- retention rate of teachers in the profession improves;
- the program provides a pool of candidates for a school district.

VIDEO 1.2

The participants in this PDS program demonstrate mutual respect and trust. The PDS model required *restructuring* in order to provide opportunities for interns to be in the school setting for longer periods of time. Time in the school needed to be balanced with requirements for university coursework. The school district and university personnel involved in the PDS program identified the *commitment of time, energy, and resources* involved in building and sustaining a successful PDS program.

Characteristics which made the partnership effective for the PDS interns included seeing the school year from start to end, opportunities to become part of the school culture, increasing responsibility in the classroom, and opportunities to work on skills such as time management. Interns in the program were considered by the school district and university to be better prepared for the challenges of their own classroom.

Characteristics which made the program effective for mentor teachers included the opportunity to challenge oneself to be a better teacher and to reflect on teaching practice and how to make it better. Characteristics which made the program effective for P–12 students included having an extra person in the classroom who cares about them and mentors co-teaching with interns.

VIDEO 2.1

The mentor is discussing an important issue about the intern's professionalism that could negatively impact her reputation and could cause her placement to be terminated.

- The *amount* of feedback provided in the conference is appropriate as the mentor focuses on one issue with the intern.
- The mentor focuses on a *specific* issue that is *relevant* to the intern's professional growth. The subject of the conference is of immediate importance to the intern.
- The mentor maintains a *positive tone* during the conference.
- The mentor models *active listening skills* by listening to the intern's feelings and responding appropriately.
- The intern is involved in identifying how she will solve the problem.
- There is a *climate of trust* that has been created between the mentor and intern as evidenced by the intern's willingness to share her feelings and frustration with the mentor.
- The mentor demonstrates *positive regard* for the intern by articulating his respect and confidence in the intern during the conference.

VIDEO 2.2

The mentor is discussing a problem with the intern's relationship with a student in the class that could negatively impact his success with this student and with other students with whom the intern will be working.

- The *amount* of feedback provided in the conference is appropriate as the mentor focuses on one issue with the intern.
- The mentor focuses on a *specific* issue that is *relevant* to the intern's professional growth.

- The topic of the conference is of immediate importance to the intern and will affect his success in working with students in the classroom.
- The mentor maintains a *positive tone* during the conference.
- The mentor models *active listening skills* by listening to the intern's feelings and ideas the intern has for working more effectively with the student and responding appropriately
- There is a *climate of trust* that has been created between the mentor and intern as evidenced by the intern's willingness to share her feelings and frustration with the mentor.
- The mentor demonstrates *positive regard* for the intern by articulating his respect and confidence in the intern during the conference.
- The mentor summarizes the conference and helps the intern reflect on what he has learned about himself as a teacher.

VIDEO 3.1

In the mentor teacher training session, the facilitator provides the group with an opportunity to become familiar with the lesson evaluation form they will be using to assess interns in their classroom and gives them an opportunity to practice using the form. Using the lesson from a popular television show kept interest high and reduced the concern of the mentors. The facilitator encouraged engagement in the activity by providing an opportunity for the mentors to work on the task by themselves and then to share their results in pairs or groups of three. The time allocated to the individual practice and group discussion is important because the mentors need time to work on the task. However, if too much work time is provided, mentors will become restless and it may be more difficult to engage them again when the next part of the activity begins. Active engagement occurs when the mentors have the opportunity to share their ideas in small groups before some of the mentors share with the whole group.

VIDEO 3.2

In the summative conference, the intern identified the following challenges in working in two different classrooms and grade levels:

- planning;
- differences in student achievement;
- meeting the needs of students with differences in student achievement; and
- meeting the needs of students from different backgrounds.

The intern identified the following teaching strategies as effective ones she had used:

- hands-on activities;
- manipulatives;
- cooperative learning; and
- lesson planning.

The intern identified important things she had learned from her clinical experiences:

- meeting the needs of diverse students;
- she is positive and excited about teaching;
- importance of being well organized;
- importance of building positive relationships with students; and
- importance of a safe and supportive classroom climate.

VIDEO 4.1

During the beginning conference with the intern, the mentor teacher demonstrated friendliness, warm regard, and active listening. Topics the mentor encouraged the intern to discuss included the following:

- family, where the intern had lived;
- how the intern selected the university and teacher education program;
- why the intern had chosen the grade level in which she would be doing her internship;
- experiences the intern had; and
- concerns and questions that the intern had about the internship experience.

The mentor demonstrated warm regard by telling the intern how helpful the experiences she had would be in her internship. The mentor demonstrated empathy by telling the intern about the expectations of his mentor teacher in one of his clinical experiences. The mentor shared information about his classroom and approach to teaching which included the following:

- mentioning some of the topics that would be covered in the transitional year of third grade;
- the importance of making school a positive experience for the students;
- promoting student security;

- encouraging the students to take risks and to feel that it is acceptable to make mistakes;
- promoting creativity; and
- letting the intern know that the principal supported the approach of the mentor teacher.

VIDEO 4.2

In the ending conference with the intern, the mentor facilitates the intern's reflection and discussion with open-ended questions such as:

- What has gone well during your experience?
- What was your greatest challenge?
- What will you remember most?

The intern demonstrates her ability to reflect on her teaching by

- discussing strategies she used to make learning fun and exciting for the student;
- identifying how she used pre and post test data to determine the effectiveness of her instruction;
- discussing her initial concerns with discipline and how she became more confident;
- identifying the importance of earning the respect of the students; and
- discussing how she was excited that students shared products made at school with their parents.

The mentor provides professional guidance to the intern by

- making suggestions to help the intern get the most out of her long term substitute assignment which will follow her internship;
- encouraging the intern to be flexible when considering possible grade levels to teach;
- encouraging the intern to work on her placement file and to keep in touch with the university placement office; and
- reassuring the intern to reduce her concern if she does not find a job right away.

The mentor teacher identified specific strengths of the intern that would be included on her final evaluation which included the following:

- planning;
- ability to be proactive by anticipating possible problems and concerns;
- classroom control; and
- earning the respect of students and family members.

There was congruence between the intern's reflection on her teaching strengths and the mentor's evaluation of the intern.

VIDEO 5.1

The mentor teacher states the objectives for the conference, demonstrates active listening skills, and uses positive body language effectively during the conference.

Clarifying questions the supervisor asks include

- Tell me one thing that went well in your lesson.
- What do you think the students liked about the lesson?
- What was something that went just as you planned during your lesson?
- What was something that went differently than you planned?
- What would you do differently next time?

VIDEO 5.2

The mentor teacher reinforces:

- the intern's calm and relaxing voice;
- the intern's lesson plan; and
- the intern's use of her math bulletin board during the lesson.

The mentor asks two clarifying questions:

- What do you think you learned about yourself as a teacher?
- What other questions do you have about the lesson today?

The intern and mentor brainstormed strategies for including a math practice as part of the lesson.

VIDEO 6.1

By actively listening to the intern, the supervisor helps the intern to identify some of the concerns he has about meeting the learning needs of students in his diverse classroom. Some of the strategies that the supervisor could suggest are

- building a positive relationship with the students in the classroom;
- visiting with the students to understand the idioms they use;
- cooperative and collaborative activities which promote student interaction;
- teaching strategies which promote student engagement;
- connecting learning to student experiences and interests;
- appropriately differentiating instruction to meet the needs of students; and
- actively checking for student understanding while teaching using every pupil response strategies.

VIDEO 6.2

The supervisor encourages the intern to reflect on some of the challenges posed by the students in her diverse classroom. Some of the challenges the intern identifies are

- wide range of student abilities in the classroom;
- behavior issues, some students seek attention;
- differences in background and home environment; and
- parents who work hard at a tough job every day and may not have time and energy to be actively involved in the school.

Using open-ended, probing questions, the supervisor encourages the student to reflect on the strategies she uses which are effective in working with students in her diverse classroom. Some of the strategies she identifies are

- ignoring minor misbehavior when appropriate;
- establishing a positive rapport with the students;
- understanding the background of the students;
- using activities which appeal to different learning styles;
- demonstrating energy and enthusiasm; and
- having clear and consistent expectations for the students.

The supervisor reinforces appropriate classroom management strategies he observed in the intern's lesson:

- proximity;
- "teacher voice" (volume, expression, and authority);
- ignoring minor misbehavior;
- private reminders; and
- redirecting.

VIDEO 7.1

The supervisor establishes a positive tone with the intern by reinforcing appropriate teaching behaviors and decisions during the lesson which included

- step-by-step lesson;
- correct use of technology;
- eye contact with students;
- flexibility, let students keep their homework to study for the test; and
- caught mistake and corrected it.

The supervisor asks clarifying questions which included

- How would you have taught the lesson differently?
- What changes would you make if you were to teach this lesson again?
- What kind of positive feedback do you give the students?

The supervisor's positive tone and clarifying questions helped the intern identify two concerns he wanted to work on:

- Some students are left out during the lesson.
- The intern does not know the names of the students in the class.

The supervisor tells the intern what he will be looking for in the next lesson:

- lesson plan with questions constructed in advance;
- positive verbal feedback to students;
- no errors in math; and
- appropriate interactions with female students, especially at beginning of the lesson.

VIDEO 7.2

Examples of the six conferencing principles which were used in the video are provided at the end of the video segment.

VIDEO 8.1

The intern demonstrates that she is an excellent intern because she can reflect on her teaching and identify strengths and areas to work on which included

- planning different learning activities for each of the centers;
- using feedback from the students for planning;
- using a variety of instructional strategies to meet student needs including colors, number sponges, letting students make appropriate choices of the activity they would like to do;
- evidence of careful planning to identify what comes next in the instructional sequence; and
- awareness that transition time from rug to tables was too long.

In addition to asking clarifying questions that encouraged the intern's reflection, the supervisor also reinforced specific behaviors from the lesson which included

- use of redirection;
- providing examples of positive reinforcement and feedback used by the intern in the lesson;
- positive interactions and conversations with students in small groups at the center; and
- letting students choose one of the activities they wanted to do.

VIDEO 8.2

In this video, you can observe that the intern in the conference is an excellent intern because she is actively involved in the conference, writes down ideas to try from the conference, and is able to brainstorm strategies with the supervisor. Some of the strategies the supervisor uses to get the intern actively involved in reflecting on her lesson are

- positive tone which is encouraging and nurturing;
- use of snapshots from the iPad to highlight specific events from the lesson to discuss;
- reinforcing ideas that the intern came up with for improving her lesson; and
- suggesting ideas for the intern to try in future lessons.

VIDEO 9.1

The principal identifies benefits of the PDS program to the interns, to the teachers at his school, to the students at his school, and to the school.

- Interns benefit from getting real-world experience doing the job they want to do.
- Interns benefit from assuming responsibilities they will have in their own classrooms.
- Interns keep mentor teachers "on their toes."
- Mentor teachers need to be more reflective.
- Interns are sometimes able to "click" with an individual student better than the mentor teacher.
- Another pair of hands helps individual students and the whole class.
- The PDS program is especially helpful to a small, rural school.
- The program demonstrates the school's commitment to excellence.

VIDEO 10.1

The facilitator encourages active involvement while participants are defining a struggling intern by

- getting the participants out of their seats;
- using a tennis ball passed around by participants to encourage everyone to talk;
- small groups to promote more talking by individuals and active listening;
- groups sharing with the whole group; and
- facilitator positively reinforces participant's ideas: "That's a good one," "That's another good one," "All right."

VIDEO 10.2

In this video, the facilitator uses a Kahoot game to check for participant's understanding of the assessments used in working with PDS interns.

Incorporating a technology activity in a game format promotes interest and involvement with the participants. Additional information and benefits of using the Kahoot strategy can be found at https://getkahoot.com/support/faq/.

This activity required all participants to have a device to access the game. Connecting each device to the game was frustrating for some of the participants and required the facilitator to be able to assist with technical problems. Facilitators should have a plan in case technology does not work as expected.

VIDEO 10.3

This activity was a concluding activity that occurred at the end of the training session. Active involvement energized the mentors and ended the training session by emphasizing the importance of the mentor teacher to the success of the intern.

The mentors were actively involved during the activity by

- writing ideas about interns;
- working in small groups to use their idea cards to build a structure;
- writing ideas about how mentors support interns;
- working in small groups to build a structure that was taller than the structure without support; and
- celebrating their success in building the taller structure (interns with mentor support).

Critical thinking was encouraged by

- thinking about the needs of interns;
- thinking about the ways mentors support interns;
- comparing ideas with other mentors in the small group; and
- building a model of the mentor's role in supporting the intern.

Appendix 2

Observable Instructional Behaviors to Reinforce

ANALYZING BEHAVIORS

1. The intern determines appropriate objectives for student learning.

   Observable behaviors:

   The intern aligns the objective with the appropriate standard.
   The intern communicates the objective of the lesson to students.
   The student intern designs appropriate plans for teaching that indicate appropriate objectives for student learning.
   The intern communicates objectives for learning to the mentor teacher and to the university supervisor.

2. The intern's instruction provides evidence of appropriate diagnosis of student learning needs.

   Observable behaviors:

   Students are working at activities at appropriate levels of difficulty.
   Students are answering questions correctly.
   Students are expending effort to learn and are successful.

3. The intern's instruction shows evidence of appropriate analysis of the learning task.

   Observable behaviors:

   Learning tasks are sequenced appropriately to facilitate student understanding.
   The intern reteaches or moves ahead in the learning sequence as needed.

The intern provides appropriate scaffolding and differentiation so that all students can be successful.

Transitions between learning activities are smooth and logical.

PRESCRIBING BEHAVIORS

1. The intern groups students to facilitate student learning.

   Observable behaviors:

   A variety of instructional groupings are used.
   Student groups change as learning tasks change.
   Cooperative and collaborative learning groups are used appropriately.
   The intern monitors groups while students work together.
   Students are on task during group activities.
   The intern teaches the appropriate social and communication skills so that students can be successful when working in groups.

2. The intern facilitates critical thinking, creative thinking, and problem solving.

   Observable behaviors:

   Students are challenged to apply what is learned to their own lives.
   Students are required to compare, contrast, and categorize when appropriate.
   Student creativity is encouraged.
   Students are encouraged to support their ideas with evidence from their learning.

3. The intern relates learning activities to the objective.

   Observable behaviors:

   Connections between learning activities and objectives are clear.
   Appropriate review helps students understand how previous learning relates to a particular objective.
   The intern paces instruction effectively.
   The intern helps students make connections between what they are learning and student experiences.
   The intern helps students make connections with previous learning.
   The intern helps students make connections with the real world.

Appendix 2

DETERMINING STRATEGIES

1. The intern's lessons are structured to promote student understanding and remembering.

   Observable behaviors:

   The intern presents information, gives directions, and responds to student questions clearly.
   The intern uses effective examples.
   The intern asks questions that promote student thought.
   Appropriate wait time and prompts are used to promote student engagement.
   Every pupil response strategies are used to promote student engagement.

2. The intern motivates student involvement and interest.

   Observable behaviors:

   All students have the opportunity to experience success. Students are actively engaged in learning.
   The intern is positive and enthusiastic about students and what is being taught.
   The intern emphasizes positive outcomes of learning.
   The intern provides appropriate feedback to students about their learning.
   The intern uses activities that appeal to different multiple intelligences when teaching.

3. The student teacher uses varied instructional activities and strategies.

   Observable behaviors:

   Learning activities involve students with appropriate reading, writing, listening, speaking, and viewing experiences.
   Technology is appropriately integrated into instructional activities.
   Critical thinking and problem solving are encouraged.
   Pictures and other visual stimuli are appropriately used.
   Movement opportunities including appropriate brain breaks are provided for students.
   Music is appropriately integrated into instruction.
   Students have the opportunity to work with others.
   Students are encouraged to think about their own feelings and opinions about what is being learned.

4. The intern demonstrates effective classroom management.

Observable behaviors:

The intern builds and promotes a caring classroom community.
   The intern builds positive, nurturing relationships with students.
   Expectations for behavior are clear and consistent.
   Positive reinforcement and positive feedback encourage appropriate behavior and attitudes.
   The intern responds appropriately to minor misbehavior.
   The intern is aware of what students are doing during instruction and work periods.
   The intern treats all students equitably.

LESSON DESIGN

1. The intern focuses students appropriately for instruction.

Observable behaviors:

The intern checks for student understanding of previously learned material.
   Smooth transitions are made from one activity to another.
   Student interest and attention are engaged.

2. The student teacher provides appropriate instruction to students.

Observable behaviors:

The intern provides appropriate input to students.
   Learning is modeled for students.
   Instruction proceeds at an appropriate pace.
   Appropriate closure is used to summarize the lesson before ending.

3. The intern checks for student understanding.

Observable behaviors:

The intern uses responses from student groups to check for student understanding.
   The intern checks for student understanding while teaching using a variety of strategies.
   The intern responds appropriately to student confusion.
   The intern makes appropriate teaching decisions based on student feedback.

4. The intern provides appropriate opportunities for students to practice new learning.

   Observable behaviors:

   The intern moves around the room checking student work and providing help as needed.

   The intern uses strategies which allow students to check their own progress when appropriate.

   Cooperative and collaborative learning groups are appropriately used and monitored.

   Appropriate differentiation is provided so all students are engaged and successful.

   Independent practice is assigned only after students have been successful in guided practice. Assessment.

1. The intern utilizes a variety of assessment strategies.

   Observable behavior:

   Students are provided with opportunities to create products that demonstrate their learning.

   Students are provided with opportunities to make appropriate choices about how to demonstrate their learning.

   The intern uses a rubric or marking guide to observe during in-class discussion and activities.

   Portfolios of student work and other strategies which promote student self-evaluation are used.

   Pre-assessment results are compared to post-assessment results after learning activities have taken place.

   Interns utilize triangulation of assessment data to assure learning has taken place.

   Adapted with permission from *Clinical Instruction and Supervision for Accountability*, 2nd ed., by Lawrence Lyman, Alfred P. Wilson, C. Kent Garhart, Max O. Heim, and Wynona O. Winn (Dubuque, Iowa: Kendall/Hunt, 1987).

Appendix 3

Example of a Professional Development School Agreement

The purpose of this agreement is to outline relevant policies and procedures for elementary Professional Development Schools (PDS), which provide clinical teaching experiences for _____ University elementary teacher education students at (school site or sites) in _____ Unified School District. All policies and agreements contained in the student teaching agreement previously approved between the District and the University remain in effect.

INTERN RESPONSIBILITIES

Each intern who is assigned to a Professional Development School site will have met all requirements for admission to Teacher Education at _____ University. Principals and staff members from PDS school sites will be invited to participate in the interview process for intern candidates and the principal and mentor teacher have the right to approve all assignments of interns. The intern will provide the PDS school site with a valid student teaching certificate issued by _____ University in compliance with the state Department of Education, a valid health certificate completed in compliance with the state Department of Health and Environment, and background check documentation in compliance with the state Department of Education.

All interns are subject to University, College, and Department policies including the Policy on Student Ethics and Professionalism and Procedures of Due Process for Early Termination of an Off-Campus Teacher Education Assignment. Copies of these policies and other relevant information concerning interns can be found in the Professional Development Schools Policy and Procedures Book which is provided to interns, mentor teachers, and principals at each PDS site.

Interns are expected to comply with school and district policies and regulations, exhibit professional dispositions and behaviors, actively participate in school district and university professional development opportunities as appropriate, and demonstrate commitment to professional growth as stated in the university's Conceptual Framework.

PROFESSIONAL DEVELOPMENT SCHOOL COORDINATORS

A _____ University staff member will be assigned as coordinator for each Professional Development School site. Coordinators will

1. clearly communicate program goals and objectives for the PDS program to mentor teachers, building administrators, and district administrators;
2. clearly communicate PDS goals, objectives, and policies to interns;
3. clearly communicate time lines for required assignments, observations, and activities to interns;
4. effectively coordinate the Teacher Education program outcomes;
5. effectively coordinate university faculty classes and presentation schedules for interns;
6. effectively coordinate additional learning opportunities for interns as appropriate;
7. observe and supervise interns during the first semester of their PDS experience;
8. observe and supervise interns during the student teaching semester, providing student teaching assessment and documentation;
9. conduct conferences with interns and mentors on a regular basis;
10. work effectively one-on-one to answer questions about individual interns and PDS goals and objectives; and
11. work collaboratively with the building principal to ensure that the needs of the university, the student intern and the building are met.

RESPONSIBILITIES OF THE PRINCIPAL

The principal of each Professional Development School site agrees to

1. assist in the selection of mentor teachers;
2. assist the coordinator by helping to clarity expectations for the PDS with mentor teachers, staff, parents, and interns;

3. interpret the school culture and expectations for the coordinator and interns;
4. observe interns as requested and provide feedback when schedules permit;
5. teach interns in areas of the principal's expertise;
6. serve as a liaison with central office staff; and
7. assist in presentations about the PDS program as requested to a variety of audiences.

MENTOR TEACHERS

Mentor teachers are recommended by the principal. Criteria should include at least three years of successful teaching experience, evidence of ability to work with interns, and willingness to serve as a mentor teacher. A Master's Degree is preferred.

Mentor teachers will receive reimbursement for each intern who is placed in their class for at least 16 weeks of the school year. The rate of payment is $250 per intern at the time of this agreement. Payment will be made to the mentor teacher by the university after appropriate documentation as required by the state is provided by the mentor teacher.

Mentor teachers are required to successfully complete two days of training before an intern is placed in their classroom. Reimbursement for attending training sessions at the time of this agreement is $100.

RESPONSIBILITIES OF MENTOR TEACHERS

Mentor teachers will

1. assist in the interviews of potential interns (as much as they wish to be involved);
2. help to develop initial training for interns, participate (as volunteers) in the delivery of awareness sessions and other training for interns;
3. become familiar with the outcomes expected of interns and suggest how these outcomes can best be met in PDS classrooms;
4. facilitate learning activities to assist interns in meeting expected outcomes;
5. participate in training sessions for mentor teachers;
6. model effective teaching and explain reasons for teaching decisions to interns;
7. engage interns in critical thinking to determine appropriate strategies for accomplishing desired outcomes with elementary students;

8. provide opportunities of increasing responsibility for interns to work with individual students, small groups, and the whole class;
9. assist interns in becoming reflective professionals who are ready to assume responsibility for their own classrooms;
10. assist the coordinator in assessing the effectiveness of the PDS and of the interns assigned to the mentor teacher;
11. hold weekly conferences with the intern to provide specific feedback on the intern's performance, reinforcement of areas of strength, and suggestions for improvement; and
12. demonstrate enthusiasm about teaching and a commitment to lifelong learning.

This agreement has been reviewed and approved by

_____   _____
University Representative   School District Representative

_____   _____
Date Signed   Date Signed

Appendix 4

Example of an Intern Improvement Contract

To: (intern)

Date:

Re: Performance Contract

During the concerns meeting with you, (mentor teacher), and (PDS coordinator) which was held on (date), concerns that have been expressed over the first 6 weeks of your PDS placement were discussed. The following concerns have been reported to (PDS coordinator) from a variety of people working at (PDS site) or at (University):

- accepting feedback in a negative, stressful way;
- difficulty understanding where student teaching interns fit in a public school setting;
- unable to productively observe and learn about teaching from your mentor teacher;
- writing incomplete lesson plans and being unable to identify parts of a lesson;
- difficulty implementing changes in behavior, lesson planning, professionalism after receiving feedback from supervisors;
- inappropriate responses to your mentor teacher and other professionals in the building in general conversation as well as during professional development, Professional Learning Community meetings, and planning times;
- asking inappropriate questions at an inappropriate times;
- arriving late to your PDS site;
- lack of positive attitude towards improving and growing in teaching;

- forgetting items when they are needed here at school (laptop, materials for teaching); and
- beginning two new jobs in the past two weeks.

As we discussed, these areas of concern must be improved in order for you to be successful in your PDS placement. This contract will focus on areas needing improvement and what you need to do to increase your chances for success. These areas coincide with the Teacher's College Conceptual Framework and Professional Dispositions.

Area of Concern	Connection to University Conceptual Framework and Professional Dispositions
Following directions in the classroom	Proficiency One: Provides Service to Society You have demonstrated difficulties related to professionalism. Demonstration of adequate improvement in this area will involve • punctual attendance to PDS, including arrival time of 7:30 a.m., all scheduled meetings, and PDS coursework. This will be evaluated on conference forms, mentor evaluation forms, coordinator evaluation forms, and/or instructor records; and • successfully following directions at your PDS site.
Preparedness	Proficiency One: Provides Service to Society You have demonstrated difficulties related to professionalism, including lack of preparedness for teaching experiences and bringing needed materials to the PDS site. Demonstration of adequate improvement in this area will involve • evidence of sufficient preparation is expected for all teaching experiences. This will be evaluated on conference forms, mentor evaluation forms, and/or coordinator evaluation forms; and • If you do not have adequate lesson plans to share with teachers or instructors prior to teaching, you will not be allowed to teach the lesson. As a result of the lesson not being taught, additional consequences may come from the university course instructor.
Professionalism, engagement and positive attitude	Proficiency Four: Responds to Uncertainty and Change You have demonstrated difficulties related to using effective communication techniques in order to develop a positive learning environment, including using difficulties using feedback as a positive learning opportunity. Demonstration of adequate improvement in this area will involve • appropriate comments, questions, and reactions to feedback including evidence of growth in this area. This will be evaluated on conference forms, mentor evaluation forms, and/or coordinator evaluation forms.

Quality of Lesson Plans	Proficiency Two: Applies Interdisciplinary Scholarly Knowledge You have demonstrated difficulties related to planning lesson that meet the expectations of the mentor teaching, site supervisor, and professors. Demonstration of adequate improvement in this area will involve • submitting detailed and thorough plans to the mentor teacher at least a week in advance that reflect evidence of sufficient preparation and application of what has been taught through modeling in the PDS classroom, district-level in-service sessions, and instruction in methods courses. This will be evaluated on conference forms, mentor evaluation forms, and/or coordinator evaluation forms.

ASSESSMENT OF PROGRESS

Your Progress in the Areas of Concern Will be Assessed in the Following Ways:

- Your mentor teacher will continue the weekly conference with you and document your progress or lack of progress on the identified areas of concern. Additional conferences may be added as needed to discuss and monitor your progress.
- Your coordinator will visit your PDS site at least once per full week of school to check on your progress on areas of concerns by meeting with you, your mentor teacher and your principal or grade level PLC members, and/or observing your teaching and interaction with students.
- A conference that involves the mentor, intern, and coordinator will be held during the week of your Ten Week Assessment. At this time, it will be determined if gathered documentation provides sufficient evidence of progress toward goals. If progress is demonstrated, you will continue at the PDS site and progress will continue to be evaluated on a weekly basis.

Causes for Removal from Your PDS Placement

We expect you to work hard to develop your skills and meet the expectations for the PDS program in general and the conditions of this contract specifically. Failure to make sufficient progress toward the goals outlined in this contract within the timeline described can result in termination of your PDS placement and may result in your withdrawal from the Teacher Education program.

Any act of insubordination or unprofessional/unethical behavior as documented on a weekly conference form or checklist by the mentor teacher, principal, or university PDS coordinator will result in immediate termination of your PDS placement.

If your PDS placement is terminated, you have the right to appeal this decision. Your appeal must be meet the requirements identified in the PDS Policy and Procedures Book (pages) in order to be considered.

Your signature on this contract indicates your understanding of the expectations for your performance in your PDS placement and the consequences if those expectations are not met.

Your signature does not necessarily indicate agreement with the information in this contract.

_____   _____
Intern's signature and date   PDS Coordinator's signature and date

_____   _____
Mentor Teacher's signature and date   Principal's signature and date

copy to Department Chair

Selected Bibliography

Abdal-Haqq, I. (1999). *Voices of caution: Equity issues, professional development schools: Weighing the evidence*. Thousand Oaks, CA: Corwin Press, 1999.

Anderson, R. H. and Snyder, K. J. (1996). *Clinical supervision: Coaching for higher performance*. Lanham, MD: Rowman & Littlefield.

Azwell, T. S., Foyle, H. C., Lyman, L., and Smith, N. L. (1999). *Constructing curriculum context*. Dubuque, IA: Kendall/Hunt.

Blackburn, B., Johnson-Taylor, C., and Young, E. (2004). Effective communication: The key to a successful internship experience. *Teachers as Leaders* 5(1), 2–6.

Blanchard, K. (2002). *Whale done! The power of positive relationships*. New York: Simon and Schuster.

Byrd, D. M. and McIntyre, D. J. (Eds.). (1999). *Research on professional development Schools: Teacher education yearbook VII*. Association of Teacher Educators. Thousand Oaks, CA: Corwin Press.

Campbell, J. M. (2005). *Essentials of clinical supervision*. Hoboken, NJ: John Wiley and Sons.

Caruso, J. J. (2000). Cooperating teacher and student teacher phases of development. *Young Children* 55(1), 75–81.

Caruso, J. J. (1998). What cooperating teacher case studies reveal about their phases of development as supervisors of student teachers. *European Journal of Teacher Education* 21, 1.

Charles, C. M. (2014). *Building Classroom Discipline* (11th ed.). Upper Saddle Creek, NJ: Pearson.

Clark, R. W. (1999). *Effective professional development schools*. San Francisco: Jossey-Bass, 1999.

Cooper, J. M. (1995). Supervision in teacher education. *International Encyclopedia of Teaching and Teacher Education*.

Costa, A. L. and Garmston, R. J. (1996). *Cognitive coaching: A foundation for renaissance schools*. Norwood, MA: Christopher-Gordon.

Covey, S. R. (1989). *The 7 habits of highly effective people*. New York: Simon and Schuster.

Cruickshank, D. (1987). *Reflective teaching: The preparation of students of teaching*. Reston, VA: Association of Teacher Educators.

Darling-Hammond, L. (2005). *Professional development schools: Schools for developing a profession*. New York: Teachers College Press.

Davis, B. M. (2007). *How to coach teachers who don't think like you: Using literacy strategies to coach across content areas*. Thousand Oaks, CA: Corwin Press.

Delpit, L. (1998). Language diversity and learning. In E. Lee, D. Menkart, and M. Okazawa-Rey (Eds.), *Beyond Heroes and Holidays*. Washington, DC: Network of Educators on the Americas.

Deschenes, C., Ebeling, D., and Sprague, J. (1999). *Adapting curriculum and instruction in inclusive classrooms: A teacher's desk reference*. Bloomington, IN: Center for School and Community Integration, Indiana University.

Ferrara, J. (2014). *Professional development schools: Creative solutions for educators*. Lanham, MD: Rowman & Littlefield.

Foyle, H. C. (1992). *Clinical supervision: A cooperative learning approach*. Emporia, KS: Emporia State University Printing Service.

Foyle, H. C. and Lyman, L. (2003). Mentoring your future colleagues. Presented at National Social Science Association Conference, San Francisco.

Foyle, H. C., Lyman, L., and Foyle, J. (1999). Lessons learned from a culturally, economically diverse classroom. Presented National Council for the Social Studies Annual Conference, Orlando, FL.

Foyle, H. C., Morehead, M. A., and Lyman, L. (1992). *Conferencing with student teachers: The beginning conference* (DVD). New York: Insight Media.

Foyle, H. C., Morehead, M. A., and Lyman, L. (1992). *The excellent student teacher* (DVD). New York: Insight Media.

Foyle, H. C., Morehead, M. A., and Lyman, L. (1992). *The incompetent student teacher* (DVD). New York: Insight Media.

Gall, M. D. and Acheson, K. A. (2010). *Clinical supervision and teacher development* (6th ed.). Hoboken, NJ: John Wiley & Sons.

Gardner, H. (1983). *Frames of mind: The theory of multiple Intelligences*. New York: Basic Books.

Garland, C. and Shippy, V. (1995). *Guiding clinical experiences: Effective supervision in teacher education*. New York: Ablex.

Glasser, W. (1998). *Choice theory: A new psychology of personal freedom*. New York: Harper Collins.

Glickman, C. D., Gordon, S. P., and Ross-Gordon, J. M. (2013). *SuperVision for instructional leadership: A developmental approach* (9th ed.). Boston: Allyn and Bacon.

Goleman, D. P. (2006). *Social intelligence: The new science of human relationships*. New York: Bantam Books.

Gordon, S. P. (Ed.). (2005). *Standards for instructional supervision: Enhancing Teaching and Learning*. Larchmont, NY: Eye on Education.

Hall, P. and Simeral, A. (2015). *Teach, Reflect, Learn: Building your capacity for success in the classroom*. Alexandria, VA: ASCD.

Hammond, M. (2007). Professional development schools: Synergy at its finest. *School-University Partnerships* 1(2).

Henry, M. and Weber, A. (2016). *Coaching a student teacher*. Lanham, MD: Rowman & Littlefield.

Henry, M. and Weber, A. (2016). *Evaluating a student teacher*. Lanham, MD: Rowman & Littlefield.

Henry, M. and Weber, A. (2016). *Preparing for a student teacher*. Lanham, MD: Rowman & Littlefield.

Henry, M. and Weber, A. (2016). *Supervising Student Teachers: The Professional Way* (7th ed.). Lanham, MD: Rowman & Littlefield.

Henson, K. T. (2010). *Supervision: A collaborative approach to instructional improvement*. Long Grove, IL: Waveland Press.

Hunter, M. C. and Russell, D. (1989). *Mastering coaching and supervision*. Thousand Oaks, CA: Sage Publications.

Jones, J., Schwerdtfeger, S., Roop, T., and Long, J. (2016). Trailblazing partnerships: Professional development schools in partnership with Emporia State University. *Journal of the National Association for Professional Development Schools* 9(1), 7–10.

Justen, J. E. III and McJunkin, M. (1999). Supervisor beliefs of cooperating teachers. *Teacher Educator* 34(3).

Kouzes, J, M. and Posner, B. Z. (1993). *Credibility: How leaders gain and loose it, why people demand it*. San Francisco: Jossey-Bass.

Levine, A. (2006). *Educating school teachers*. Washington, DC: The Education Schools Project.

Lopez-Real, F., Stimpson, P., and Bunton, D. (2001). Supervisory conferences: An exploration of some difficult topics. *Journal of Education for Teaching* 27(2).

Lyman, L., Leone, F., and Delgado, T. (1997). Strategies for creating and maintaining a collaborative community in a professional development school setting. Presented at Kansas University National Professional Development Schools Annual Conference, Kansas City, MO.

Lyman, L., Mann, L. A., and Patterson, M. (2007). Community college partnerships: Giving the best to students. Presented at the National Social Science Association Summer Conference, Vancouver, BC.

Lyman, L. (2000). A professor returns to the classroom in a professional development school. Presented at the National Conference of the Kansas University Professional Development Schools Alliance, Kansas City, MO. Retrieved from ERIC database (ED439095).

Lyman, L. and Foyle, H. C. (1989). Creative supervisory conferences: New wine in old skins? *Florida ASCD Journal*, 45–47.

Lyman, L. and Foyle, H. C. (1990). *Cooperative groupings for interactive learning: Students, teachers, and administrators*. Washington, DC: National Education Association.

Lyman, L. and Foyle, H. C. (1998). Facilitating collaboration in schools. *Teaching and Change* 5(3–4), 312–339.

Lyman, L. and Foyle, H. C. (2015). Collaboration to create e-textbooks for college courses. *National Social Science Technology Journal* 5(2), 5–9.

Lyman, L., Foyle, H. C., and Lyman, A. L. (2011). *Managing interactive classroom learning communities for elementary and middle school students.* El Cajon, CA: National Social Science Press.

Lyman, L., Morehead, M. A., and Foyle, H. C. (1989). Building teacher trust in supervision and evaluation. *Illinois School Research and Development* 25(2), 54–59.

Lyman, L., Wilson, A. P., Garhart, C. K., Heim, M. O., and Winn, W. O. (1987). *Clinical instruction and supervision for accountability* (2nd ed.). Dubuque, IA: Kendall/Hunt.

McClure, R. M. (1990). School improvement through colleagueship and cooperation. In L. Lyman and H. C. Foyle (Eds.), *Cooperative groupings for interactive learning: Students, teachers, and administrators.* Washington, DC: National Education Association.

McClowry, S. G. (2016). *Using what works: Elementary school classroom management.* Lanham, MD: Rowman & Littlefield.

Mann, L. A. and Lyman, L. (2007). Enhancing public school and university professional development school partnerships: The community college link. *School-University Partnerships* 1(1), 80–82.

Marzano, R. J. and Simms, J. (2012). *Coaching classroom instruction.* Bloomington, IN: Marzano Research.

Melser, N. A. (2004). The shared supervision of student teachers: Leadership, listening, and lessons learned. *Professional Educator* 26(2), 31–37.

Miller, S., Duffy, G., Rohr, J., Gasparello, R., and Mercier, S. (2005). Preparing teachers for high-poverty schools. *Educational Leadership* 62(8), 62–65.

Morehead, M. A., Foyle, H. C., and Lyman, L. (2003). *Conferences with incompetent and excellent student teachers* (DVD). Scotts Valley, CA: Create Space.

Morehead, M. A., Foyle, H. C., and Lyman, L. (2003). *Conferences with student teachers: Beginning/Ending and formative conferences* (DVD). Scotts Valley, CA: Create Space.

Morehead, M. A., Foyle, H. C., and Lyman, L. (2004). *Conferences with student teachers: Discussing diversity issues* (DVD). Scotts Valley, CA: Create Space.

Morehead, M. A., Lyman, L., and Waters, S. (1988). A model for improving student teaching supervision. *Action in Teacher Education* 10(1), 39–42.

Morehead, M. A. and Waters, S. (1987). Enhancing collegiality: A model for training cooperating teachers. *The Teacher Educator* 32(2).

National Council on Teacher Quality. (2016). *Student teaching in the United States.* Retrieved from http://www.nctq.org/dmsView/Student_Teaching_United_States_NCTQ_Report.

Obiakor, F. E. (1994). *The eight-step multicultural approach: Teaching and learning with a smile.* Dubuque, IA: Kendall/Hunt.

Pawlas, G. E. and Oliva, P. F. (2007). *Supervision for today's schools* (8th ed.). Hoboken, NJ: John Wiley & Sons.

Roberts, S. M. and Pruitt, E. Z. (2008). *Schools as professional learning communities: Collaborative activities and strategies for professional development* (2nd ed.). Thousand Oaks, CA: Corwin.

Roe, B. D., Ross, E. P., and Smith, S. H. (2009). *Student teaching and field experiences handbook* (7th ed.). Upper Saddle River, NJ: Prentice Hall.

Ross, D. L. (2002). Cooperating teachers facilitating reflective practice for student teachers in a professional development school. *Education* 122(4), 682–687.

Rubenstein, G. (2007). Confronting the crisis in teacher training: Innovative schools of education invent better ways to prep educators for the classroom. Retrieved from http://www.edutopia.org/schools-of-education.

Schwartz, W. (2001). The impact of professional development schools on the education of urban students. Retrieved from ERIC database: http://www.ericdigests.org/2001-2/urban.html.

Shulman, J. H., Sato, M., and Feiman-Nemser, S. (2006). *Mentoring teachers toward excellence: Supporting and developing highly qualified teachers.* San Francisco: Jossey-Bass.

Slick, G. A. (1995). *Making the difference for teachers: The field experience in actual practice.* Thousand Oaks, CA: Corwin Press.

Slick, S. K. (1998). A university supervisor negotiates territory and status. *Journal of Teacher Education* 49(4).

Stinson, W., Mehroff, J. H., and Thies, S. A. (1993). *Quality thematic lesson plans for classroom teachers: Movement activities for pre-k and kindergarten.* Dubuque, IA: Kendall/Hunt.

Taylor, R., Smiley, L., and Richards, S. (2014). *Exceptional students: Preparing teachers for the 21st century* (2nd ed.). Columbus, OH: McGraw-Hill Education.

Tharp, J. M. (2007). *Breaking the cycle of failed school reform: What five failed reforms tell us.* Lanham, MD: Rowman & Littlefield Education.

Tomal, D. R., Wilhite, R. K., Phillips, B., Sims, P. A., and Gibson, N. (2015). *Supervision and evaluation for learning and growth.* Lanham, MD: Rowman & Littlefield.

Vare, J. W. and Young, E. A. (2007). Perceptions of the quality of mentor teachers' supervision in professional development school and non-professional development school settings. *School-University Partnerships* 1(2), 9–18.

Voneschenbach, J. F. and Gile, W. B. (2007). Dispositions for teacher education candidates. *School-University Partnerships* 1(1), 72–79.

Wiles, J. and Bondi, J. (2004). *Supervision: A guide to practice* (6th ed.). Columbus, OH: Merrill.

Wong, H. K. and Wong, R. T. (2014). *THE classroom management book.* Mountain View, CA: Harry Wong.

Zeichner, K., Melnick, S., and Gomez, M. L. (1996). *Currents of reform in preservice teacher education.* New York: Teachers College Press.

Zepeda, S. (2012). *Instructional supervision: Applying tools and concepts.* New York: Routledge.

Index

absences, 29
accountability, 28, 41
    through assessment, 34
    through evaluation, 35–36
    through shared governance, 34–35
action research, 5
active listening skills, 18
administrative support, 3
adult learners, 121
affirmation statements, 18, 48
appreciation, 22
Ashburn, E., 81
asking questions, 18
assessment
    accountability through, 34
    decisions, 65
    of dispositions, 31
    informal, 51
    meetings for, 29
    midpoint, 49
    during PDS, 27
    self, 32–33
    of skills, *23*
    of student achievement, *77*
    of student learning, 63, 81
    from teacher work samples, 33–34
    variety of strategies for, 77, *77*, 81, 143
attendance, expectations on, 43

behavior problems, 57
best practices, 110
bias, 80–81
The Big Bang Theory, 36
body language, 18
brainstorming, 50, 66, 106
    alternative approaches designed with, 67
    hitchhiking during, 68
    on risk taking, 105
budgets, 112
building principals, 30
bullying, 82
Bunton, D., 95

Caruso, J., 89
celebration of successes, 3, 54
child abuse, suspected, 114
children, positive relationships with, 73
clarification, understanding from, 50, 64
    questions, *65*, 105–6
    strategies, 65
    university supervisors and, 66
classroom management, 63
    class on, 7
    in diverse settings, 82
    effective, 142
    resources for, *85*
Classroom Observation Guide, 7, *44*, 45

classrooms
  diverse, *84*
  P–12, 5
  physical appearance of, 79
  private space in, 20
  rules in, 41
  specific information on, 21
  university, 7
  vision for, 102
  visits to, 66, 98
classroom situations, 4, 7
clinical field experiences, 27
  changes during, 51
  conclusion of, 52
  data gathered during, 29
  final weeks of, 50
  sequencing of, 42
collaboration
  climate for, 109
  in PDS programs, 110
  planning, 47
  teacher educational analysis with, 2
collaborative partnerships, 3
community colleges
  general education at, 28
  partnerships with, 8, 35
Conceptual Framework, 32, 33
conferences, 50
  beginning, *42*
  daily, 46
  initial, *43*
  with interns, excellent, 102–3
  with interns, struggling, 94–95
  motivational, 101, 105
  parent–teacher, 51
  professional, 101, 103–4
  for reflection, 101, 104–5
  skills for, 120
  weekly, 47
  See also formative conferences; summative conferences
confidentiality, 17, 52
consumable supplies, 112
convergent questions, 68
corrective guidance, 113

counseling programs, 48
cultural factors, 74, 75
  consideration of, 79–80
  discussions of, 81
curriculum
  adaptation of, 63
  materials, 5, 41
  meetings on, 35
  restructuring, 6–7

data
  from classroom visits, 98
  from clinical field experiences, 29
  collection of, 36
  comprehensive, 28
  formative, 61
  on performance, 57
  from planning, 33
  from unaware and unskilled interns, 93
digital filing systems, 40
disagreements, 3
dispositions of teacher candidates, 28
  assessment of, 31
  examples of, 32
  observation of, 31
dissemination opportunities, 10
district policy violations, 20
divergent questions, 68
diversity, 73, 80, *84*
  classroom management and, 82
  instructional planning for, 77
  of student needs, 78
dress code, 114

Educating School Teachers (Levine), 1
Education Week, 16
Edutopia, 16
electronic textbooks, 5
elementary mathematics methods, 6
email, 69
empathy, 42
Emporia State University, 4
evaluation
  accountability through, 35–36

lesson, 61
of performance, 50
summative, 49
of training, 123, *123*
expectations, high, 17

feedback, 31
    from building principals, 30
    effective, 18–19
    from formative conferences, 59
    by mentor teachers, 30
    negative, 94, 96
    on performance, 61
    during professional
        conferences, 104
    professional growth from, 49
    quantity and quality of, 27
    receptivity to, 15
    specificity of, 48
    trust built by, 21
    from university supervisors, 35
    variety of, 52
financial resources, 110, 112
flexibility, 67
fluency, 67
formative conferences, 58, 76
    form for, *60*
    with interns, unskilled, 92
    specific feedback from, 59
    university supervisors and, 61
Fresno State University, 14
friendliness, 42
full-time teaching, 47

Gardner, Howard, 78
general education requirements, 8
    at community colleges, 28
goals
    agreement on, 2
    educational, 41
    for improvement, 49
grades, 52
graduates, 10
grant writing, 5
group-building activities, *74*, 75, 140

impact of, 121
opportunities from, 79
Gutierrez, C., 111

Hermosa Heights Elementary
    School, 110
higher-level cognition, 63, 76
hitchhiking, 68

identifying strengths, 22
improvement
    areas of, 33
    goals for, 49
    strategies for, 91
improvement plans, 90, 98
    example of, 149–52
incentives, 31
instructional behaviors, 47
    analyzing, 63
    congruent with effective
        teaching, 58
    reinforcement of, 62, 64
    student focus and, 142
    student learning and, 62
instructional planning, 41
    diversity factor in, 77
instructional problems, 57
instructional strategies, 19
intelligence areas
    body-kinesthetic, 78
    logical, 78
    verbal, 78
    visual, 79
interns, excellent, 106–7
    characteristics of, 101, *102*
    conferencing with, 102–3
    self-criticism by, 106
    working with, 105–6
interns, struggling, 89, 97
    causes of, 90
    conferences with, 94–95
    key issues for, 95
    resistance from, 96
    university supervisors and, 120
    unsatisfactory performance of, 94

interns, unaware
  data from, 93
  defensive, 93
  remediation of, 92
interns, unskilled, 90
  data from, 93
  formative conferences with, 92
  work examples for, 91
interns, unwilling, 93
inter-rater reliability, 121
interviews, 13, *14*, 46

Justen, J. E. III, 106

Kansas Future Teacher Academy, 9
knowledge base, 102
Kouzes, J, M., 15

learning activities, 63
learning environment, positive, 15, 17
learning experiences, developmentally
  appropriate, 78
lesson evaluations, 61
lesson plans, 5, 42, 44
  effective, 63
  emailing of, 69
  for student learning, 18
  written, 50
Levine, Arthur, 1
liberal arts faculty, 28
listening, 42
Lopez-Real, F., 95
lower-level cognitive responses, 76
lower socioeconomic situations, 80

Mannisto, P., 101
maturity, 16
McClure, Robert, 6
McJunkin, M., 106
meaningful learning, 81
media center, 112
meetings
  for assessment, 29
  on curriculum, 35
  first, 43
  midterm, 28

mentor teachers
  feedback from, 30
  roles of, 29
  selection of, 112–14
methods classes, 4, 28
midterm meetings, 28
minority teachers, 8, 9
monitoring, 84, 85
multicultural themes, 74, 81
music, 79, 141
mutual respect, 3, 111

National Association for
  Professional Development
  Schools, 3
National Council for Accreditation of
  Teacher Education, 31
National Council on Teacher Quality, 1
National State Teachers of the Year, 9
National Teacher Hall of Fame, 9
negative attitudes, 17
New Mexico State University, 110
nonthreatening behaviors, 82

observation, 7, *8*, 46, 66
  of dispositions, 31
  guided, 45, 74
  of interpersonal skills, 28
  journal for, 59, 61
  scheduled, 116
  of students, 75
  of university supervisor, 91
openness, 42
organization, 40
orientation, 44
  meetings for, 97, 115
originality, 67

paper-and-pencil tasks, 78
paperwork, 40
parents and guardians, 46
  informing of, 114
partnerships, productive, 111
  characteristics of, 2–3
  between educators, 1
  strategies for sustaining, 10

PDS. *See* Professional Development Schools
PDS Policy and Procedures Book, 13
Peltokallio, L., 101
people search activity, 122, *122*
performance
　data collection on, 57
　evaluation of, 50
　feedback on, 61
　student achievement inhibited by, 58
　unsatisfactory, 94
pet peeves, 21
placement
　file, 52
　new, 97
　office, 52
　potential problems before, 14
　removal from, 61
planning
　data from, 33
　long-range, 41
　skills, *14*
playground duty, 114
policy and procedures manuals, 44
portfolios, 80
positive communication, 15
positive confrontation, 98
positive relationships, 22–23
　with children, 73
positive tone, 21
Posner, B. Z., 15
prescribing behaviors, 140
principals, 116
　best practices knowledge of, 110
　input from, 112
　orientation meeting with, 115
　PDS role of, 109
　responsibilities of, 109, 115
prioritizing, 40
Professional Development Councils, 123
Professional Development Schools (PDS), 3–5
　assessment during, 27
　collaboration in, 110
　desired outcomes of, partnerships, *4*
　example agreement of, 145–48

　principals role in, 109
　real-world setting of, 6
　sites for, 124
professional growth, 51, 105
　from feedback, 49
　signals of, 59
　skills for, 5, 102
　from training, 124
professionalism
　attitude for, 17
　conferences on, 101, 103–4
　demonstrations of, 103
professional model, 83
professional relationships, 15
program standards, 34
public suggestions, 16
punctuality, expectations on, 43, 46
pupil–teacher ratio, 111

ratings, 7, *8*
real life examples, 122
recalibration, 121, 125
record keeping, 28, 59, 61
recruitment, 9
reference letter, 52–54
reflection, 40
　benefits of, 106
　conferences for, 101, 104–5
　emphasis on, 104
　journals for, 80
　practice of, 102
reinforcement, 61–62
　communication of, 22
　of instructional behaviors, 62, 64
　positive, 19, 48, *83*
relaxation, 40
relinquishing control, 16
remediation, 68–69, 98
　continual failure after, 90
　of interns, unaware, 92
Renaissance Group, 33
Renaissance Teacher Work Sample, 33
response opportunities, 76
responsibility
　basic, 40
　giving back of, 52

increasing amounts of, 48
  out-of-school, 39
  of principals, 109, 115
  to students, 98
  of university faculty, 27
responsible risk takers, 105
restructuring, 3
rituals and ceremonies, 10

scheduling, 29
school culture, 21
Science, Technology, Engineering, and Mathematics (STEM), 102
seating charts, 75
second language learners, 78, 80, 111
self-centered focus, 51
shared governance, accountability through, 34–35
sink or swim model, 46–47
skills, 5
  assessing, *23*
  in communication, 17–18, 120
  conferencing, 120
  interpersonal, 16, 28
  planning, *14*
  for professional growth, 5, 102
  specialized, 120–21
  supervision, *14*, 119
social fee, 114
special-needs students, 73
staff bathrooms, 112
stages of development, 89
standardized test scores, 80
STEM. *See* Science, Technology, Engineering, and Mathematics
Stimpson, P., 95
stress, 41
structured interviews, *45*
  with students, 73
student achievement, 58
  assessment of, *77*
student learning, 22, 58, 64, 111
  assessment for, 63, 81
  detriment to, 98
  diagnosis of needs, 139
  instructional behaviors and, 62

  lesson plans for, 18
  objectives for, 139
  teacher work samples for, 33
students
  checking work of, 76
  equitable opportunities for, 76
  ethnically diverse, 80
  focus of, 142
  high expectations for, 81
  inappropriate behaviors of, 82
  misbehavior of, 48
  nonverbal cues by, 79
  observation of, 75
  off-task behavior of, 91
  responsibility to, 98
  structured interviews with, 73
summative conferences, 58
  evaluation from, 59
  final, 61
supervision, 30, 57
  congruency and discrepancy model of, 57
  nondirective approach to, 106
  skills, *14*, 119
  walk through, 115

Talvitie, U., 101
teacher council, 35
teacher education
  collaborative analysis of, 2
  national reports on, 1
teacher shortages, 90
teacher work samples, 33–34
teaching behaviors, *84*, 85
  equitable, 75
teaching context, 15
teaching decisions, 4
  explanations of, 15, 16
"teaching hospital," 4
teaching performance, 32
teaching strategies, variety of, 78
technology, 79
  appropriate integration of, 141
  changes in, 41
  strategies for, 111
tenure, 124

time management, 39, 40
training
 advanced, 125
 content for beginning, *120*
 evaluation form for, 123, *123*
 incentives for, 123–24
 objectives for, 121
 people search activity for, *122*
 professional growth from, 124
 programs for, 31
 in specialized skills, 120–21
 of university supervisors, 119
travel stipend, 31, 123
trust, 67
 climate of, 20
 feedback building of, 21

understanding, checking for, 40
university credit, 124
university faculty, 5
 responsibility of, 27

university representatives, visits by, 66
university supervisors, 21, 30, 64
 availability of, 45
 clarification and, 66
 feedback from, 35
 formative conferences and, 61
 interns, struggling and, 120
 observation of, 91
 training for, 119
 travel stipend for, 31

video recordings, 50–51, 106

warm regard, 42
Wong, Harry, 79
work ethic, 13
workload, 20
written activities, overuse of, 78

Zeichner, K., 81, 82
Zimpher, N., 81

About the Authors

Lawrence Lyman is professor of elementary education at Emporia State University where he serves as co-director of the Professional Development School program and facilitates mentor teacher training since 1988. He has served as an elementary school teacher, elementary principal, and university department chairperson.

Harvey C. Foyle is professor of education in the Instructional Design & Performance Technology Department at Baker University (KS). He is a former high school social studies teacher and departmental chairperson. His university experience includes curriculum planning/instruction, social studies education, history/political science, computer technology, and student teacher supervision. He holds the rank of emeritus professor at Emporia State University (KS).

Michael A. Morehead is associate dean at Burrell College of Osteopathic Medicine and Dean Emeritus at New Mexico State University. He is a former secondary school teacher and administrator. Dr. Morehead coordinated student teaching programs for more than fourteen years at Northern Arizona University and Emporia State University. During this time, he coordinated the assignment of more than four thousand student teachers.

Sara Schwerdtfeger is an assistant professor and co-director of the Professional Development School program in the Elementary Education/ Early Childhood/ Special Education Department at Emporia State University. She currently teaches methods courses, supervises PDS interns, and teaches graduate courses in the Instructional Specialist: STEM program. As a former elementary school teacher, Sara taught over sixteen years and has mentored many interns. She has her Master's degree in elementary education as well as graduate endorsements in teacher leadership and building leadership/administration from Emporia State University and is a Ph.D. candidate in curriculum and instruction with an emphasis in Mathematics Education at Kansas State University.

Allyson L. Lyman is an assistant middle school principal in the Emporia Public Schools. She is a former elementary teacher. During her years as teacher, she served as a mentor teacher for many interns. She also graduated from the nationally recognized elementary education program at Emporia State University where she was an intern in the Professional Development Schools Program. She earned her Master's degree in school leadership from Emporia State University.

www.ingramcontent.com/pod-product-compliance
Lightning Source LLC
Chambersburg PA
CBHW020830020526
44115CB00029B/100